A SHORT AND HAPPY GUIDE TO BEING A LAWYER

AF704151

By

Kenney F. Hegland

James E. Rogers Professor of Law, Emeritus

Paul D. Bennett

Clinical Professor of Law

Series Editor

Paula A. Franzese

Peter W. Rodino Professor of Law
Seton Hall University School of Law

WEST®

A Thomson Reuters business

Mat #41218507

Thomson Reuters created this publication to provide you with accurate and authoritative information concerning the subject matter covered. However, this publication was not necessarily prepared by persons licensed to practice law in a particular jurisdiction. Thomson Reuters does not render legal or other professional advice, and this publication is not a substitute for the advice of an attorney. If you require legal or other expert advice, you should seek the services of a competent attorney or other professional.

©2012 Thomson Reuters

610 Opperman Drive
St. Paul, MN 55123
1–800–313–9378

Printed in the United States of America

ISBN: 978–0–314–27879–1

Put me in Coach—I'm ready to play today,
Look at me, I can be Centerfield.
—John Fogerty

This book is dedicated to the Coaches
—Clinicians

Acknowledgments

Once we start it would be hard to stop. We have learned so much from colleagues, from scholars who have written in the field, and from our students who have repeatedly insisted that we articulate our insights, "So, why was that cross *better*?" Barbara Sattler edited the book and made terrific suggestions, Alex Lane offered spiffy advice, and Paul Kealey, Taylor Green, and Mohyeddin Abdulaziz, put up with us. Special thanks to Judy Parker who is wonderful to work with. This book is better thanks to Professor Paula Franzese, the Yoda of Property Law.

Why Short and Happy?

> *I started with a girl with some flowers in her hand walking in a room in a country house. Sentences simply grew into paragraphs, and paragraphs became a chapter. I knew I had started a novel but I didn't know what novel it was.*

Ian McEwan on writing his novel *Atonement*

Maybe you have, or soon will, walk across a room with a law diploma in your hand. You will know you have started a career but you won't know what that career will be. Lucky you. We are absolutely jealous.

Forget the lawyer jokes. John Adams, our first Vice President and second President, was a prime mover, perhaps *the* prime mover, behind the American Revolution. No John Adams, no American Revolution, and you would still be studying the English estate system, *O to X for life, remainder in fee to Y.* What was Adam's first love? Political theorist? Revolutionary? President? No. Lawyer!

> *Now to what higher object, to what greater character, can any mortal aspire than to be possessed of all this knowledge, well digested and ready at command, to assist the feeble and friendless, to discountenance the haughty and lawless, to procure the redress of wrongs, the advancement of right, to assert and maintain liberty and virtue, to discourage and abolish tyranny and vice?*

Sure, there will be disappointments and difficulties. Jobs are hard to find, clients can be demanding and unappreciative, and opponents, jerks. But remember all you have and will accomplish and that you are part of a grand profession, you and John Adams.

This is a "short and happy guide" to being a lawyer. We will cover a lot of territory—interviewing, counseling, discovery, negotiating, and trying lawsuits. Others have books on these topics; what gives?

We provide a quick overview of the basic techniques. This format leads to quick reading; don't leave home without a sense of how your various tasks fit together: knowing something of cross-examination will inform client interviewing and knowing something of negotiation will make you a better counselor. Further this format allows for easy review when the time comes. Before your first trial there is no time to read a lengthy book on trial practice.

This is to take nothing away from the books of these topics. Read them. The more you learn, the more you know, the more you can learn—what once was puzzling suddenly makes sense. One of the best trial lawyers we know attends every trial workshop she can, even those for beginners. She *always* learns something new.

But are basic techniques enough? They'll get you by. Dr. Steven Rosenberg, then Chief Surgeon of the National Cancer Institute, wrote of his early days:

> *Even if I lacked the specific skill to perform particular operations, such skills can be readily developed if one knows the basic techniques. Judgment is harder to develop.*

How to develop judgment?

Practice. Before you send an email, cross-exam a witness, respond to an offer, realize that you have choice to make and that all choices entail "inconvenient facts," things that go dump in the night. What can go wrong and why aren't other ways the better choice? After you sent your email, questioned the witness, responded to the offer, pause to ask yourself how your choice worked out. Self reflection is the best teacher.

Keep up on current events—all of us, clients, opponents, judges, are buffeted by news, sports and, unfortunately, teenage dress and nose rings. If you love intellectual problems you loved law school; if you love people, you'll love practice. To learn about people, read novels. They're a great break from the hurly burly, even though you don't get CLE credit.

That's the short of it: we'll cover the basics. How about the "happy"? Men and women in serious black suits may suggest, "This is a serious profession; we're talking prisons, divorce, money. No room for happy, no room for humor." These folks are morticians (or should be).

We love logical loops, philosophical puzzles, and bad jokes. Some, resenting distractions, might wish that we would simply get directly to our point, no matter how dull, no matter how obvious. If you are one of them, you have picked up the wrong book.

> *"Dost thou think, because thou art virtuous, there shall be no more cake and ale?"*

Sir Toby, Twelfth Night

Fred Rodell, a law professor at Yale no less, once wrote an article with a spiffy title: *Goodbye to Law Reviews.*

> *There are two things wrong with almost all legal writing. One is style. The other is content. That, I think, covers the ground. Readers like a dash of pepper or a dash of salt along with their information. They won't get any seasoning if lawyers can help it. Lawyers would rather be dignified and ignored.*

We won't be ignored. We want to help you become a better lawyer. We'll wear lampshades and throw dignity to the wind. This book should be dedicated to Sir Toby and Professor Rodell; in fact, the entire "Short and Happy" series should be.

"Live Greatly in the Law"

Oliver Wendell Holmes so urged his listeners. In our cynical world the audience would snicker. Was a time we weren't mere hired guns, hawking our wares on late night television, being the butt of a thousand and one jokes. Think Atticus Finch, the lawyer as a pillar of the community, someone to turn to in sad times for advice and counsel, and someone who would, when ill winds blew, stand tall in the pursuit of justice.

> *A lawyer leaves his office late at night. He is accosted by a mugger.*
>
> *"Your money or your life."*
>
> *The lawyer hesitates. "Answer me. Your money or your life."*
>
> *"It just hit me. I have no life."*

Are things going to be that bad? Absolutely not! You have chosen a tough profession; you have chosen a wonderful profession. The intellectual challenges are invigorating. You won't see 40 cases of flu each day and write the same prescription. A good friend, a lawyer, is married to a doctor. "Lawyer parties are so much better. Doctors talk about their investments; lawyers talk about their cases."

But the intellectual challenges are not the best part. The best part are the people. Sure, your colleagues can be jerks but they are bright and seldom bored or boring. As for your clients, you will be involved in their varied lives at critical times. You will learn so much about how people live, how they cope, and what they dream. People will come to you for your help. Caring for others is a deeply satisfying endeavor; practicing law is more than a job, it is a privilege.

So what gets in the way of "the thrill of it all"? Stress and choosing the wrong job.

Stress

Unreasonable deadlines, ungraceful clients, complicated cases, high expectations, sleazy adversaries. If you are not stressed you don't understand the situation.

Stress can be highly functional. You have all been there. You are daydreaming in class. Suddenly you hear your name with a question attached. Boom, your brain kicks in. You rise to the occasion. You score. Our brains are hardwired to react to immediate stress by producing adrenaline and cortisol that push our brains and bodies into high gear. Cognition improves. Reactions improve. *We feel the rush.*

In the long run, however, chronic stress becomes distress–lack of sleep, irritability, depression, and poor decision-making. Too much cortisol rushed too often to the brain over an extended period of time can disconnect neural networks and even kill brain cells. Chronic stress can hurt memory, concentration, immune systems, and can mess with your emotions. *Ouch!* And by the way, your emotions really do matter.

You may not know you are stressed (but your blood pressure will). Periodic medical checkups are essential. Short of meds and counseling, find someone safe to talk to and ask for help if you need it. Sleep, exercise, non-law activities are always helpful. For non-law activities realize that *non-profit boards* are always in the market for lawyers. So too Little League. Such activities, by the way, help your business.

Stress may be caused by overwork. Take a close look at what you do each day. What tasks can be delegated? Learn to say "no". Give up on being perfect—turn in a brief even if it isn't your best work. Don't meet sleaze with sleaze, that is a downward tunnel; meet sleaze by being a better lawyer. Avoid clients becoming ungrateful by staying in touch with them, not promising too much, and explaining why things may not be going better. Finally, come to peace with yourself. You're a lawyer, you've done good, and you don't have to be President.

Finding the right job

> *Success is not the key to happiness. Happiness is the key to success. If you love what you are doing, you will be successful.*
>
> Albert Schweizer

So, what is it that you like to do? "Like" isn't the only word we could use. We could use "attuned to", "satisfied by", "derive meaning from", "look forward to" or "motivated by". But "like" works for short and happy.

Do you like to plan or do you like to react?

Do you like working with people or do you like working alone?

Do you like to work with books or do you like to be with people?

Most transaction lawyers like planning. They like to anticipate problems and solve them before they arise. Most litigators like to solve problems after the crisis. How can we fix this mess? Most plaintiff's lawyers like to build a case. Most defense lawyers like to take things apart. What do you like?

We don't mean to say that all planners become transaction lawyers and vice versa. Lawyers don't fit into neat boxes any more than any other people. But the questions are useful. *Are you motivated by money? Competition? Intellectual challenge? People? Ideology? All of the above? None of the above?*

Are these all the questions? Nope. You know who you are. You figure out the right questions for you.

And don't be afraid to experiment.

> *"I wanted to be a trial lawyer but a client was a contractor. That's all I do."*

> *"I never wanted to go to court but a business client got a DUI. That's all I do."*

Many lawyers, maybe most lawyers, change jobs several times before settling in. Career mobility is one of the great advantages of the law. A law career is a buffet. Try stuff and figure out what you like. Julia Child advised:

> *"Moderation. Small helpings. Sample a little bit of everything. These are the secrets of happiness and good health."*

How do you know if you've landed successfully? Sure, the money will be a factor as will the kinds of cases you handle but most important is whether you like going to work in the morning. Not every morning, but some mornings, it should be "Great, I get to go to work today!"

Now let's get busy.

Introduction

The Lawyer's Search for Happiness

By Paula Franzese
Peter W. Rodino, Professor of Law, Seton Hall Law School

Prof. Franzese is the author of A Short and Happy Guide to Property (West, 2011), and Editor of the Short and Happy series.

This book is a jewelbox of gems. In it, Professors Kenney Hegland and Paul Bennett, accomplished practitioners and teachers, capture the magic and promise of our craft. In these pages, you will find a blueprint for success in law and life. Beyond the many nuts and bolts contained inside, whether you are (or plan to be) a solo practitioner, partner in a firm, public interest attorney, in-house counsel or anything in between, you will discover a perspective for finding within that venture perhaps the most elusive of experiences—joy.

A happy lawyer is a productive agent of change for the better, even if the improvement is simply one of attitude. Here are just a few essential guideposts to consider as you find yourself immersed in the life of the law:

- **Lighten up.** Angels fly because they take themselves lightly. We tend to take ourselves too seriously, allowing our egos to get in the way of desirable outcomes and meaningful exchange. As my dear friend and colleague Andrea Schwartz, Esq., often says, "Your ego is not your amigo." The real challenge, then, as you ascend as a practitioner of substance and expertise, is to *honor the art in you, and not you in the art.* It is not about us, no matter how exceptional we perceive ourselves to be. It is about our clients and their struggles. It is about the aims of justice, and achieving those for the greatest good.
- **Wisdom and compassion are indivisible.** Excellence cannot persist in the absence of kindness. On my computer screen I have these words from Karl Llewellyn, legal genius and parent of the Uniform Commercial Code: *"Compassion without technique is a mess. But technique without compassion is a menace."* We need both expertise and empathy.

Respect intelligence, but respect decency even more. At the end of each day, the people that you encounter probably won't remember too much about what you achieved, but they will remember how you made them feel.

- **Success is not the key to happiness. Happiness is the "key to success."** Albert Schweitzer was right. Gratitude is the way to joy. No matter the adversity, indignities and incivilities that a life in the trenches can be subjected to, we remain in charge of our reactions. A grateful heart doesn't have the room or the capacity to respond to meanness in kind. Cruelty comes from weakness. Gentleness comes from strength. A spirit rich in appreciation for everything and everyone twinkles. It is impervious to the slings and arrows, because it knows that the boomerang effect will only return those to their sender. We get what we give. And in a world of infinite possibilities, we don't get what we want. We get what we *are*. A grateful person will always have more to be thankful about. A cynic will always have lots to complain about.
- **Love the law, and treat it as if you love it.** So urged Justice Cardozo in his address to NYU Law School's first graduating class. Even if you have to fake it until you make it, love our craft. Persist in loving the law, even when it doesn't love you back. As I said to my beautiful teenage son Michael as he endured his first heartbreak at the behest of the young lady he had thought was the love of his life, "We are who and what we love, not who or what loves us. And love is always a choice. Choose it, again and again and again, and remember that the love part, at least at first, is easy. It is your capacity to persist in loving, in keeping your heart open, and in choosing to remember that a broken heart has more room, that will ready you for the stuff of greatness." Alan Cohen wrote that "the cracked places let in the light." Be grateful for the imperfections, your own and those of others, and even for the disappointments. Let in the light of your humanness and very human shortcomings. Forgive others' theirs.
- **What we think about and talk about most expands**. However we define the legal profession and our place in it, it will be just like that. Hence, we must take care to seek out the good and to speak out the good. Be a passionate praiser. Be guided by what you admire and not by what you detest. Look for the high-minded, read about the heroic, and talk about the acts of courage, big and small, that you observe.

Speak the truth directly and with compassionate honesty, not brutal honesty. There is too much brutality in the world. Let the words that you choose promote understanding. Don't participate in gossip, mean-spirited humor or name-calling. Avoid sarcasm, which is weakness in disguise.

- **Avoid labels.** Kierkegaard was right when he said, "If you label me, you negate me." The imposition of a label (as in, my "opponent," "adversary," "liberal," "conservative" and so on), shuts the door to the world of variations, possibilities and surprises that the withholding of judgments lets in.
- **We are not what we are called. We are what we answer to.** It is essential that we take the time to answer for ourselves the question, "Who do we think we are?" Otherwise, the world will jump in to answer for us. We are not automatons, technocrats or hired guns. We are champions of the underdog, a voice for those who have yet to find their own, guarantors of due process and crusaders for justice. Those are the designations that we should be answering to.
- **The time to be happy is right now.** We are accustomed to delayed gratification and self-sacrifice for a greater good. Yet, in actuality, happiness is not the end but *the means* to that greater good. Your joy serves the world, and gives others' permission to express theirs. Every atrocity in the course of human history has been committed by people who were miserable.

In one of the *Don Juan* allegories, Carlos Castaneda wrote, "The trouble with you is, you think you have time." That may be the trouble with all of us. The time is now to remember who we are and what we stand for, and to show up, really show up, as a force for the good.

My wish is that you wield the instrument of the law to close the gap between what is and what ought to be. Use your hard-earned expertise to give people hope. Because when all is said and done, if you can do that, well, that is something to be really happy about.

Table of Contents

Page

ACKNOWLEDGMENTS v
WHY SHORT AND HAPPY? vii
LIVE GREATLY IN THE LAW xi
INTRODUCTION xv

Part One. Skills for All Seasons **1**
Advice for All Seasons 1
Problem Solving 6
Telling Stories 9
Lies, Memories and Mistakes 14

Part Two. Practice Skills **21**
Interviewing Clients 21
Counseling 26
Investigation: Be Skeptical 30
Taking and Defending Depositions 34
Negotiation 40
Making Deals 47
Legal Writing 51

Part Three. Courtroom Skills **57**
Oral Argument 57
Part A: Trial Preparation 61
Trial Preview and Checklist 61
Planning (Backwards) and Strategic Choices 66
Prepare Your Witnesses 71
Practice Your Questions 74
Problem Witnesses 80
Objections 83
Part B: Game Day 88
Jury Selection, Pretrial Motions and Where to Sit 88
Opening Statement 92
Direct: Telling Stories 97
Cross Examination 105
Closing Argument, No Conversation 112

That's All Folks!

A SHORT AND HAPPY GUIDE TO BEING A LAWYER

Part One
SKILLS FOR ALL SEASONS

ADVICE FOR ALL SEASONS

Reputation trumps class standing

No one will care that you didn't win Moot Court, make Law Review, or weren't in the top 10%. But they will care about who you are: are you ethical, do you work hard, overcharge clients, keep your promises? They gossip. You will be tempted weekly, if not daily, to tell a little lie, cut a small corner, not to line your own pocket, but rather to advance a client's just cause, in the words of Shakespeare, "To do a great right, do a little wrong." Little wrongs add up and you have thrown away what matters most.

Be nice

A diner snarls "More butter!"

"Sorry Sir, I am to give only two tabs"

"Do you know who I am? I am a United States Senator."

"Glad to meet you Senator. Do you know who I am? I'm the man with the butter."

Never talk down to court personnel, secretaries, or waiters. If common decency is not sufficient reason, these folks have the butter.

We would condemn pomposity but those who are won't listen. But if this quote from Shakespeare seems to be about you, pause.

I am Sir Oracle and when I speak let no dog bark.

Prepare but don't stick to your script

As long as we are talking butter, an actor asks her director, "Last night, in the second act, when I asked for the butter, I got a terrific laugh. Tonight, nothing. What happened?"

"Last night you asked for the butter. Tonight you asked for the laugh."

You can never prepare too much, otherwise you are lost. Plans however can become stale. The script may get in the way of spontaneity; you must be able to react. To quote General Eisenhower after Normandy, "In preparing for battle I have always found that plans are useless, but planning is indispensable."

Think it out before; think about it after

Step (1) Before you do anything, ask: ***What am I trying to do?*** Define your goal; make a plan.

Step (2) Review the plan and ask: ***Will this help me do what I am trying to do?*** If you are still on track, go for it. If not, revise.

Step (3) When you're done, ask yourself: ***Did I accomplish what I set out to do? If so, why; if not, why not?*** File that answer under Something important I learned today.

Step (4) ***"What did I learn today that will help me as a person and as a lawyer?"***

Put it in writing

Instructing dogs is iffy.

"OK, Toby, I've had it. Stay out of the garbage. Or else."

Toby hears: *"Blah, blah, Toby, blah, blah, blah, blah."*

All communication is an iffy thing. One way to increase the odds is to put it in writing. Whether it is a settlement agreement, an opinion letter to a client or confirming a lunch date, put it in writing and send it out.

Write clearly and neatly . . . and proofread. How you present information may be just as important as the facts that you present. One insurance adjustor gives higher settlements if the demand letter is professional. Avoid typos, poor grammar, and *"It was the beast of times."*

Read the Statutes and the Rules

When you a new to an area spend an evening reading the annotated statutes in that area. Periodically reread them, not only because laws change but because the more you know about a subject, the more subtleties jump out. This is the same reason one rereads police reports and witness statements during trial.

Pursue the facts

Instead of "law practice" call it "fact practice." On law exams you can get away with "The question is whether Jones knew of the offer at the time." In practice you have to answer that question. Momentarily we will talk about solving problems and telling stories; you can't do either without a firm grasp on the facts. Unfortunately facts can be distorted by memory, interest, and lies. We will spend a lot of time on these topics.

Teach yourself and write your thoughts

After you interview a witness, negotiate a case, counsel a client don't rush to do the next thing. Review! What went well? What went badly? How would you do it differently? Most of what we do is motivated and to change behavior we must address the root causes. If you made a mistake, why?

We think too fast and too superficially. Write your thoughts—writing slows the mind so that you see new relationships and have new insights.

Take criticism gracefully; in fact, seek it out

No one likes being criticized. Realize your teachers and colleagues are on your side and are trying to help you become better. It may hurt. Suck it up. It could have been worse. And if they say nothing at all, ask them for critique. Expect contradictory advice on such matters as to how to interview a client, how to conduct a negotiation, how to write a brief. This simply shows that the practice of law is an art—listen, evaluate, and then adopt your own style.

Listen and get comfortable with Silence

Listen, not to frame your next question or argument, but to understand what the other person is saying. We'll talk later about "active listening" which requires you to reflect back what the other person has said. It's hard to do as it requires a shift in our attention, from how *we* will respond to what *they* are saying. It's an essential skill.

Another essential skill is being able to remain silent when it seems your turn to talk. A judge asks you a question, don't mumble what first comes to mind, pause and think; an adversary does not react to your offer, don't jump in with another one; a client falls silent, don't jump in with a question (maybe the client is mulling over an important insight).

Admit mistakes

Denial is generally worse than the misdeed. If you don't grasp that, go into politics.

All choices are wrong, some are worse than others

Argue liability before damages? Take the sting out? Don't make the first offer? Maybe. Maybe not. There are always choices. All entail problems. Before you do anything recognize that you have a choice—if an alternative doesn't come to mind, think; and always have a reason for the choice you made ("I always do it that way" or "Professor X says to do it this way and she wrote a book!" is seldom a good reason).

Your case is not all that good

Remember first year Moot Court. Alas, you were dismayed when you drew the losing side only to realize, after much research, you had a sure winner. As someone you never heard of once said:

A man's interest distorts his judgment far oftener than it corrupts his heart.

Update clients

One of the chief complaints about lawyers is that they fail to keep their clients informed. Return all calls and emails before you go home even to say, "Nothing new."

Essential Admissions (they get easier with practice)

"I need help." "I was wrong." "I'm sorry."

You are not treating a disease

This is a nursing school mantra but works well for us as well. You are representing people, not cases. Your little voice of doom and dour predictions will eventually calm down and you will become comfortable being a lawyer. The danger is that you might become too comfortable. C.K. Chesterton wrote:

> *The horrible thing about all legal officials, even the best, about all judges, magistrates, barristers, detectives, and policemen, is not that they are wicked, (some of them are good), not that they are stupid, (some of them are quite intelligent), it is simply that they have got used to it.*

It may be your hundredth case but it's your client's first.

PROBLEM SOLVING

To find good solutions, find easier problems

"To stop malaria, let's figure out ways to kill the mosquitoes." But wait!

> *"Malaria can be reduced by drugs that attack the parasite, by procedures that prevent mosquitoes from biting man, by insecticides that poison mosquitoes, or by agricultural practices that interfere with their breeding."* René Dubos, *Mirage of Health*

Every problem is caused by the confluence of many problems; some will be easier to solve than others. Rather than trying to kill the mosquitoes, it may be easier to interfere with their breeding. The real problem isn't malaria, it's that malaria kills people. If you can find a cure or vaccination you can leave the mosquitoes alone.

Your client has been served with an unlawful detainer complaint for non-payment of rent. Your first response would be to think of ways to defeat the eviction action. But wait!

What other factors have converged to make the unlawful detainer a problem? Obviously the client is having a hard time making payments, maybe because he can't afford the rent, maybe because he lost his job, maybe because he frequents the track. These might be easier to solve. But wait!

Isn't the real problem that the client may not have a place to live? This opens up new possibilities: help him find alternative housing or build him a new house (bear with us).

Before you start swatting mosquitoes or filing motions, have you found the easiest problem to solve? What gets in the way? Labels, your inner critic, and your tendencies.

Avoid labels

To deal with the blooming confusion of life we label. But once we label we overlook other labels that might be better. Conceptions shape perceptions. Test subjects, given a metal ball, a string and a nail, were asked to make a pendulum. No problem. They used the metal ball as a hammer. The experiment was then repeated, this time with the metal ball labeled "Pendulum Ball." This stumped many. Looking at the ball, they saw "pendulum ball," not "potential hammer."

When we see a drug addict, if we see "criminal" we will consider penalties; if we see "patient" we will consider medical interventions; and, if we see "misfit" we will consider social programs. If we see our landlord/tenant problem as "Unlawful Detainer," we will treat it differently than if we see "Needs Housing."

Silence your Inner Critic: That is a Stupid Idea

Judgment blocks creativity. Creativity is a fluid, almost unwilled process: while thinking of a problem, solutions suddenly "pop" into your head. Ideas are the river; judgment—this is a "stupid" idea; this one is "sound"—is the dam.

Building your client a house is a stupid idea. This is a good reason to reject it but does not excuse never *considering* it. Ideas beget ideas. If you can't build your client a house, perhaps your client can. There are many "self-help" housing projects. By prematurely rejecting a silly idea—without turning it over in your head—you may never discover the sound idea that lies beneath it.

To avoid premature judgment, play with finding new problems and new solutions. Write your thoughts. Writing slows your mind to allow creativity. One thinks, "Build a house; no that's silly" in a split second. Writing takes time. Write "Build a house" and another idea will pop into your head: "If I can't build him a house, maybe he can."

Be Aware of your Tendencies

Avoid routine approaches to problems. Some lawyers seek to increase the client's *economic* position; others seek to vindicate the client's "*rights*," and still others seek to reduce the client's *conflict* position. If you find that you are treating all of your cases in the same way, rethink.

Be Aware of Your Emotions

According to the Harvard Decision Science Laboratory, emotion pathways in the brain engage more rapidly than cognitive pathways. Emotions are influencing our decision-making whether we know it or not, whether we like it or not, and before we even have a conscious thought. Awareness helps.

Consider the Opposite

A scientist once posited that no experiment can be complete until the scientist considers whether the opposite could be true. Not bad advice for a lawyer. Considering the opposite increases the possibilities.

The Paradox of Dogma

Without a little dogma we would never get anywhere; we would give up too early. In science no theory fits all the observed data—that everyone who has the virus doesn't get the disease doesn't mean the virus doesn't cause the disease. Rather than giving up on the virus and looking for another cause (which won't explain everything either), scientists should figure out why the virus doesn't present in every case.

But dogma can become ugly; science can become alchemy. It becomes increasingly difficult to throw over your theory and begin anew. Playing cards were shown, one at a time, to the subject. There were a few anomalies, like a red 3 of Clubs. Often these anomalies were *not* noticed, the card being incorrectly identified as either the 3 of Clubs or as the 3 of Hearts or Diamonds.

Once you have a theory of your case, you are in danger of overlooking inconvenient facts, judicial language that hurts, and, in the case of statutes, the wee words, like "not".

On big issues no one concedes. Scientists aren't any better than the rest of us. Max Planke wrote "You never convince your scientific opponents. Eventually they die out."

We have an investment in what we believe. In Nick Horney's book, *How To Be Good*, the husband tells his wife that a man laid hands upon him and cured his chronic pain. "So this guy's a healer. Like a faith healer."

> *"It's not hard to grasp that someone is a healer, after all: he touches you, you feel better, you go home. What is there to understand? It's just that everything else you have ever believed about life becomes compromised as a result."*

Tolstoy wrote:

> *"Whatever position a man may hold, he is certain to take that view of human life in general which will make his own activity seem important and good. Men instinctively mix only with those who accept their view of life and of their place in it. This surprises us when thieves boast of their adroitness, prostitutes flaunt their shame, murderers gloat over their cruelty. We are surprised, however, only because the circle, the sphere, of these men is limited, and principally because we are outside it."*

TELLING STORIES

"The statement of facts is not merely part of the argument, it is more often than not the argument itself."

We tend to think judicial decisions rest on precedent, policy, and, now cynically, politics. But John W. Davis, appellate lawyer extraordinaire, knew facts pushed analysis, knew the importance of story telling.

How can you tell a good one? The Supreme Court introduced a case with:

> *Defendant Paul is the Chief of Police of Louisville, Kentucky. For the purpose of alerting local area merchants to possible shoplifters who might be operating during the Christmas season, he distributed to approximately 800 merchants in the Louisville metropolitan area a "flyer" of active shoplifters. The flyer consisted of five pages of "mug shot" photos, arranged alphabetically. In approximately the center of page 2 there appeared photos and the name of the plaintiff, Edward Charles Davis III.* Paul v. Davis, 424 U.S. 693

You get a very different sense from reading a law review description.

> *Plaintiff Edward Charles Davis, a photographer for the Louisville Courier–Journal and Times, was arrested in Louisville, Kentucky, on a charge of shoplifting. He pled not guilty and was never called upon to face that charge in court. With the onset of the Christmas season, defendant Paul, the Chief of police for Louisville, prepared a five-page flyer containing the names and mug shots of "Active Shoplifters." Copies of this bulletin were distributed to merchants warning them of possible shoplifters.*

How does the Supreme Court's story create sympathy for the defendant while the law review's has one rooting for the plaintiff? Both tell the same story, neither resorts to flowery language nor explicitly call for justice.

Point of View

The Supreme Court tells the story from the viewpoint of the defendant Chief of Police. What would he immediately tell us? That he is the Chief of Police and was engaged in a noble effort: alerting local merchants of possible shoplifters. It was, after all, Christmas. The protagonist in the law review version is the plaintiff, Mr. Davis. What would he tell us? That he has a job, and that he was never convicted of shoplifting.

Once we have picked a side we tend to view the world through their eyes. Neither the Justice who wrote *Davis*, nor the law student writer, were *consciously* slanting their statement of facts. The slanting occurred unconsciously once they became sympathetic to one of the parties. When we takes sides, the facts (and eventually the law) *tend* to line up in support; some facts jump out, others retreat.

There is a famous gestalt drawing containing the images of both a young woman and an elderly woman. Some see the young woman, some see the older one. *Both are there.* The Supreme Court Justice saw a well-meaning cop at risk, while the law review writer saw an innocent man seeking just compensation. Both are there.

Your first task is to *know* your client's viewpoint. What would your client say? Listen carefully to how your client views the various events that occurred. Tell the jury the story as the client lived it. But also be aware how a jury will hear it. Your job is to translate your client's point of view into language that the jury will appreciate and understand.

Beyond point of view, good story telling consists of strong themes, colorful language, and specific facts.

The Importance of Opening Lines and Themes

"It was the best of times, it was the worst of times."

Novelists work hard on their opening lines. They want to grab interest, state a theme, get things moving. They would never, ever, open: "This is a story about the French Revolution," or "This is an appeal from the Superior Court in Toledo."

Begin with pizzazz. State your basic theme.

> *"This case is about a hard working police officer who was doing his best to protect small business owners from shoplifting. He mistakenly put a man's photo in the middle of a flyer showing shoplifters. Now he's being sued."*

> *"Mr. Davis, a photographer for a local newspaper, found his 'mug shot' posted all over town." He awoke one morning to find himself turned into a hideous shoplifter.*

Most cases come down to very simple propositions: "One man, one vote," "Our Constitution is color blind," "No one should profit from his own fraud." What is the one thing you want your audience to take away? That's your theme.

The Power of Language

Words hypnotize. Early common law courts were hostile to arbitration because an early judge labeled it as an attempt to *"oust"* the jurisdiction of the courts. Well, no one is going to put up with that. Of course, had arbitration been characterized *"parties freely choosing an alternative forum"* it would have been embraced. Words matter.

"Alerted" versus *"Warned"*

"Possible Shoplifters" versus *"Active Shoplifters"*

"Photo" versus *"mug shot"*

The Power of Emotion

Even benign words can trigger emotions that can color how a jury will hear your client's story. People who remember the Challenger tragedy will react differently to the simple word "O-ring" than people who did not. Jurors' own emotions will filter what they hear and how they react to what you tell them. As you tell the story, think about how the jurors will be feeling.

Specifics, not Abstractions

In *The Merchant of Venice*, Shylock comes to claim his "pound of flesh." Asked why he would have Antonio's flesh rather than his money, Shylock responds

He hath disgraced me, and hindered me half a million;
laughed at my losses, mocked my gains, scorned my nation,
thwarted my bargains, cooled my friends, heated
mine enemies, and what's his reason? I am a Jew.

Hath not a Jew eyes? Hath not a Jew hands,
organs, dimensions, senses, affections, passions?
fed with the same food, hurt with the same weapons,
subject to the same diseases, healed by the
same means, warmed and cooled by the same
winter and summer, as a Christian is? If you prick
us, do we not bleed? If you tickle us, do we not
laugh? If you poison us, do we not die?

Forget the rhythm of the language; we ain't Shakespeare. But note Shylock's specifics: losses, gains, friends, enemies, eyes, hands, organs, dimensions, senses, affections, passions, food, weapons, diseases, healing, warmed, cooled, bleed, laugh and die. We don't have to have anyone tell us that Antonio was a bigot; we know he was because we know what he *did*.

Stress specifics, not abstractions; talk nouns and verbs, not adjectives and adverbs. If justice on your side, proclaiming it in a grand sweeping manner won't convince. Facts will. Again, review the two statements in *Davis*. Neither statement resorted to adjectives or pleas and yet each convinced the reader of very different positions.

Cement your stories with physical events. What did people *do*? What *happened*?

> "The lecture was boring; two people went to sleep, one walked out."
>
> "The movie was scary; I couldn't sleep for two nights."
>
> "The sound was quite loud; it woke the baby."
>
> "We feel sorry for ourselves; we go without meat and curse the bread."
>
> "He was depressed; he put a bullet through his head."

Dealing with Inconvenient Facts

Even novelists have to deal with inconvenient facts. Mark Twain described how *Puddinhead Wilson* changed as he was writing it, leaving characters "stranded, idle, forgotten, and permanently useless." He had one of the boys go out to stone a cat, fall in the well and drown. He was going to get rid of some of the others that way but realized that wouldn't work: the readers might get suspicious and "it was not a large well and would not hold any more anyway."

While you need not bring up every inconvenient fact (which would make your story one long apology), never omit key ones: *your opponent won't*. Had the Supreme Court version never told me that Davis had not been convicted I would feel betrayed and would lose all confidence in the story and its author.

Brevity

> *In the whole composition there should be no word written, of which the tendency, direct or indirect, is not one of pre-established design.*
>
> Edgar Allen Poe

We can't demand that much discipline of ourselves but, hey, give the rest of us a break. Lawyers talk too much. Rather than thinking about few pithy points and colorful phrases you'll use in your story, *write it out*. Then edit.

1. Does it tell the story from your client's standpoint?

2. Can you find words with more punch?

3. Can you strike points to make it shorter, more focused?

4. Does it include details and facts, avoiding adverb, adjectives, and shameless pleas for justice?

5. In your quest to win, have you omitted key facts that your opponent will ram down your throat?

6. *Does it end?*

The last point needs emphasis. Many appellate arguments, many jury arguments, simply go on and on as the lawyer desperately flogs away, trying to think of something better than "That's all Folks."

That's all folks.

LIES, MEMORIES AND MISTAKES

Whatever the essence of truth and falsity, and whatever the sources of error in our lives, one such source is surely the human agent, receiving and giving out information, intentionally deflecting, withholding, even distorting at times.

Sissela Bok, *Lying: Moral Choices in Public Life*.

Lies

We are are not the most reliable of reporters. We are not trained observers and we all are biased. We have suspect memories. Perhaps we were deceived and sometimes we lie. Sometimes, we simply tell you what we think you want to hear. "Great class, Professor." "Yes, I do like your hat."

One way to prevent lies is to convince people that they can't get away with them, that you are interviewing them not to *find out* what happened but to simply *confirm* what happened. Bob Woodward of Watergate fame would approach a witness with:

> *" I basically know the facts. I just want to confirm a few points."*

Another way is to ask why the person might lie and deal with it. Some witnesses may lie to help your client; the worst thing to happen is to put on the favorable testimony only to have your opponent expose the lie on cross.

> *"I know you want to help my client but the way to help is to tell me the truth, even if it is bad."*

Clients may lie out of shame—the truth is too embarrassing, or that, if you know it, you won't help them, or lying is one of their survival skills. Or that maybe, just maybe, they are worried you're a gossip. It is your job to create enough trust that it will minimize the lies.

> *"I know we are getting into a touchy area. Everything you tell me is covered by the attorney/client privilege which means I won't tell anyone. And, no matter what happened, I'm here to help you and there's no reason to be embarrassed as I have heard everything."*

Of course there are exceptions to privilege. If your client makes a creditable threat to kill Barney (and is older than say 8), the privilege no longer applies. If a client starts talking about planning illegal activity or involving you in a fraud, stop them and discuss what disclosures are not protected.

Once the lie is told, it's hard to dislodge. If you think your *client* is lying you must confront them in a kind, gentle manner.

> *"That doesn't make a lot of sense to me. I don't think a jury will buy it. Let's move on and come back to it later."*

Memories

> *When I was about four a man wearing a baseball cap tried to kidnap me. We were at the Mall, near the escalator, he grabbed my hand. I had an ice cream in the other. My brother screamed and he ran off. I'll never forget it.*

This never happened yet the narrator believes it. His older brother told him that it did.

Suggestion can create false memories. In one study residents were asked if they recalled watching the TV footage of a plane crashing a few months before. There was no such footage but many recalled seeing it. Books, movies, friends corrupt our memories. Self-suggestion can too. If the person has told his story to many others, his current rendition might not be based on his original impressions but on what he told others.

> *"Have you seen TV stories on this? Heard what other witnesses said? Told your story to others?"*

Consider the profound, yet liberating, implications of this. Maybe all your memories of your lousy childhood *never* happened—they really happened to luckless characters in movies, Halloween stories, and Hans Christian Anderson Fairy Tales. You are free . . . nothing bad ever happened to you! Didn't we promise a happy book?

But the narrator seemed so *certain*. Had he said, "I'm pretty sure this happened" we would be suspicious. However Professor Daniel Schacter, in *The Seven Sins of Memory*, points out that witnesses who seem highly confident are frequently no more accurate than witnesses who express less confidence. *Certainty* is more of an indication of personality than of accuracy—some are dogmatic, others are tentative. But what about the details? Aren't they indicative of truthfulness? Not necessarily.

It is possible to confuse a situation which did happen with one that did not. Perhaps our narrator was once at a Mall, near the escalator, eating an ice cream and saw a man with a baseball cap. When his brother tells him of the kidnap attempt, the narrator sees all of the details. A witness sees a man at the grocery store and, a few minutes later, at the drug store, sees someone who looks like the man commit a robbery. By unconsciously switching the scenes, the witness will describe the innocent defendant perfectly. In both cases we are awash in details. This is known as *misattribution*.

Another source of false details is *filler*. The human mind is a wondrous thing: what it doesn't know it makes up. Once our narrator believes the kidnap, in a flash the mind fills in the details. Filler is constant. When you read, "We were at the Mall, near the escalator," you saw it happening in your *mall*, not my mall, the one I saw when I was writing. We witness a scene and form a conclusion—"Ratner threw the first punch." Once we have that conclusion we unconsciously fill in supporting details (the surprised look on the victim's face). "How do I know Ratner threw the first punch? Well, for one, I saw the surprised look on the victim's face."

Insisting on details will not disclose mistakes caused by filler; indeed, that may backfire and make the memory even more real to the witness.

Let's turn to situations where events that did happen are recalled inaccurately. Errors can be caused by expectation and bias. The boss will truthfully describe the pickets as "threatening," while the union organizer will truthfully describe them as "determined." Imagine the Celtics playing the Lakers in the NBA finals. Someone in green drives the lane and bangs into someone in gold. Is it a charge? We'll make a very large sports wager that—even with instant replay—Celtics fans will see it differently from Lakers fans.

Memories involving time, distance or size are suspect. In emergencies, time stands still. Recall when you first heard your name called in Contracts. Distance estimates are based mostly on size. We have a good idea how far away a person is because we have a pretty good idea of the size of people; it is hard to estimate the distances of mountains. If the identified object is larger or smaller than usual, mistakes are more frequent: basketball players are further away than they appear and small dinosaurs, regrettably, are closer than they appear.

Trial lawyers may measure the courtroom: "Was she standing about as far from you as from you to the end of the jury box?"

Even experts fall victim to faulty vision and recall. While very few scientific papers are the product of fraud, as *many as 30 percent* contain results or conclusions that are wrong or are not reproducible. In *The Transformed Cell*, Dr. Rosenberg writes:

> *Too often investigators allow themselves to be fooled.... Often a result depends on a subjective measurement, an unconscious bias can affect measurements of, say, the size of a tumor difficult to feel. Bias can also enter into the decision about which data to discard.... Investigators can easily rationalize. "The technician forgot to change the water in mouse cage number six for four days," they might say to themselves, "and that's why those mice died. So we shouldn't count them in the results."*

Mistakes

To *avoid* mistakes one must assess the situation correctly. There are factors which distort one's assessment. While we may not be the actual center of the universe, we are the center of ours. Ask a couple *"What percentage of the housework do you do?"* and the figure will be far north of 100%. This is known as the *self-serving bias*. Your clients will sincerely believe, based on the objective record, that they deserve a bigger piece of the pie.

Everyone sees through glasses colored by politics, religion, or profession, everyone it seems *but* us. It is very hard to realize that you too have certain biases which distort your judgment. Best we can advise is to fess up and then try to analyze the distortion—do you tend to see things from a particular viewpoint? Correct what you can; you will see situations better and make better decisions.

Optimism can lead to big mistakes: we tend to believe we are less likely than others to be involved in an auto accident or come down with an illness; smokers tend to believe that they are less likely than other smokers to get heart disease and lung cancer. Favorable facts jump out, unfavorable remain hidden. We forget the time we inadvertently ran the red light. Expect your clients may be overestimating the chances of a happy outcome; a large part of lawyering is helping clients get a truer understanding of their situation.

Another distorting factor is *extremism aversion*. We shy away from extreme decisions even if they are the best. We don't like extremes, or "extremists," of whatever stripe. Seldom do we order the most expensive meal or the cheapest. A car dealer offers the "*super* deluxe" package, not primarily to sell it, but to make the "deluxe" package a middle choice. We walk away, not thinking of the thousands we have spent, but the hundreds we have saved. Between alternatives, most people seek a compromise. This impacts negotiation and trial strategy: initial positions should tend toward exaggeration. But, then again there is the *fairness bias.*

We want to be fair, or at least not be treated unfairly, and this may trump self-interest. In the Ultimatum Game a player is given $10. That player must give some of the money to the second player. If the second player accepts it, both keep what they have; if the second player rejects it, all of the money is returned. Bargaining is not permitted. It seems that Player Two would accept any amount offered by Player One, say $1. However, Player Two's sense of fairness trumps and the $1 spurned. Offers of less than 20% are routinely rejected, much to the chagrin of the Law and Economics Movement. No matter your bargaining strength, unless you present your offer as fair, you face an uphill battle.

Another factor is the *hindsight bias*—the sense that what happened was inevitable. We're big sports fan and, after a big game, it seems to us that the result was inevitable. "We never really had a chance; they're too quick." We will likely recall all the factors pointing to the eventual outcome, forgetting entirely the rush of contingencies.

As the English historian C. V. Wedgewood pointed out:

> *History is lived forward but it is written in retrospect. We know the end before we consider the beginning and we can never capture what it was to know the beginning only.*

To capture what it was to know the beginning only, when you first interview a client, write down some of the phases and metaphor he uses to describe his situation.

A disturbing (or liberating) illustration of hindsight (or perhaps of filler) comes from split brain research. Once epileptic seizures were controlled by cutting corpus callosum that connects the right and left hemispheres of the brain to prevent the seizure from moving from one lobe to the other. This had no effect on daily life, but did allow for interesting experiments: whispering in one ear communicated with one side of the brain without the other side knowing. The subject was told to walk across the room when a certain command was given. The command was given and the subject began to walk across the room.

"Where are you going?" The verbal side hadn't a clue. But still it answered:

"To get a glass of water."

We don't run because we are scared, we are scared because we run. So taught the psychologist William James. Stepping off a curb and hearing the squeal of brakes, you jump back automatically; thereafter comes the fear. Maybe all action *precedes* motivation.

The happy news is that all the bad things you think happened to you maybe didn't. The perplexing news is that maybe your life is simply a series of random events, with your mind in a constant state of catch up, making up motivations in order to maintain the illusion that you really are in control.

Whether this is good or bad news we leave to you.

Part Two
PRACTICE SKILLS

INTERVIEWING CLIENTS

Common Errors

Jumping in too early

Eventually you will tell your client's story, perhaps to an insurance adjustor, or a prosecutor, or an opposing lawyer, or to a judge and jury. Tell it from their point of view, with their words, with their emotions. You won't get very far interrupting them with your questions, no matter how insightful. Why do we cut clients off with our profound, professor approved, questions? We think that we that professionals should be in charge, (asking questions puts one in charge), we become irritated when the client "won't get to the point," and, when the client falls silence, we rush to fill the void. How odd considering that most clients come with a purpose and want to get things off their chest right away. They need you to understand their problem. Why do clients just sit there? They may not know what is expected of them, or fear that long discussions by them will run up the bill.

> *"Simply tell me what brings you here. Take your time. We have half an hour. I probably won't be asking any questions until I get a good idea of your situation. I might jog down some notes but don't let that distract you."*

Stereotyping clients

Law school, ("What else should the plaintiff have argued?"), presents a warped view of human nature: our goals—to avoid liability, take no responsibility, and get more money. (Economists are no better.) We are shocked when a defendant says "I did cause harm and I want to make things right" or a plaintiff says, "I just want to be understood, and an apology would be nice." Don't assume your clients are typical clients with typical goals; if you do, with the questions you ask, the points you stress, you may make them so.

Avoiding unpleasant facts

Know the bad as well as the good: you will want to win, you will want to help, and you tend to avoid the bad, by shifting the conversation from unpleasant facts and leaving probing questions unasked.

Avoiding unpleasant emotions

Many of us are more comfortable with the intricacies of the Rule Against Perpetuities than we are with the emotional plight of disgruntled heirs. We are supposed to solve problems; we get shaky when the client brings up matter beyond our speciality. Don't duck. How a client feels about things, and how strongly, will impact on how you handle the case and, even if they don't, simply being listened to about things that matter builds rapport and confidence—essentials.

Ice Breaking, Rapport Building, and Advising as to Confidentially

Of course it is important to build rapport and, in some cases, to discuss attorney/client privilege, but *not* in the first five minutes. Best to start by encouraging the clients to tell you why they came and allowing the rapport to build over time as it becomes apparent that you are on their side and that you understand their situation. As to attorney/client privilege, discuss it when and if it becomes relevant.

Giving Advice

The best of advice can fall on deaf ears. When we stop talking legal jargon, we talk graduate student. We are so familiar with what we do it is easy to forget that clients likely haven't a clue. (Recall the bewilderment you felt in the first weeks of law school.) To make things still more iffy, realize that many clients will be emotionally distraught.

> *I'm going to tell you what I'm going to do and (if appropriate) what I'm not going to do. This is what I want you to do and what I don't want you to do. Please ask questions. Sometimes I'm not a clear as I should be . . At the end, I will ask you to tell me our plan.*

Predicting Outcome

Sometimes lawyers are asked to do things that can be assuredly accomplished, such as drafting a will or writing a contract. However in contested matters (civil or criminal) it is irresponsible to predict a certain outcome even though the clients will likely push for one. (The criminal lawyer who advises "I'll get you off this one and my fee, up front, is $20,000" should be disbarred.) The most you can do in the first interview is to assure clients, in words or general demeanor, that you are competent, take their matters seriously, and will work hard on their behalf.

Five Questions

In response to "How can I help you?" your client says:

"I'm divorced and raising my two small children. I just got an Eviction Notice from the landlord."

Immediately you see that the problem is the eviction notice and the solution is to defeat it. But is it?

1. *What is your problem?*

The fact that the problem fits neatly into one of our categories doesn't mean that it is the root concern of our client. Maybe the response will be, "Getting evicted," but maybe not: "I'm worried about the kids having to change schools," or "I'm worried, if I lose the apartment, I'll lose custody."

2. *What caused it?*

While we see "nonpayment of rent," our client may see more fundamental causes: "I lost my job," or "One of the kid's needed braces," or "I lost the money at the casino." Distinguish between long-term causes and immediate triggering events. ("What caused you to lose your job?")

3. *What would be a good outcome?*

Often clients will not have thought this through. In the back of his mind the father may think that staying in the apartment is his goal, being asked the question may lead him to other insights, "You know, if I just had enough time, I am sure I can find a better place nearer the kids' school."

4. *How can we solve your problem?*

Enlist your clients in thinking of solutions; they may have better ideas than you do. "Maybe I could ask my mom for a loan." Or maybe they are considering bad options: "I can get a Payday Loan."

5. *What will the other side say about this?*

If it is a contested matter, unlike a will preparation, you must probe for unfavorable information. Occasionally you must confront your client, "That doesn't make much sense to me."

Don't worry, you don't have to remember the five questions. Simply jot the key words at the top of my yellow pad ("describe problem," "causes," "best outcome," "how?" "bad stuff") and refer to them as you go along.

Client Narration and Active Listening

Down the road your client's story will become lifeless, a series of remembered and oft repeated facts and events. To make the story live, you need to recapture the immediacy of its first telling. As your client talks, jot down the phrases and metaphors first used to explain their situation.

Encourage the client to narrate, offer encouragement along the way ("This is helpful") and sit back and listen even if things tend to drift. *Active listening* is extremely helpful. It is easy to describe but difficult to do. Thomas Shaffer in *Legal Interviewing and Counseling* describes it: when the other person pauses, you say, *"You are saying THIS about THAT?"*

> *"Let him correct you if your reflection is wrong. Try to get into the feelings behind what he says; make them your own. Make the words your own; reflect what he means, in your words."*

Reflecting back what the client said assures that you understood correctly. What else can be said for the technique?

1. Most people have a powerful need to be understood. It's one of the reasons criminal defendants confess. Reflecting back conveys to your client that you understand and that you took the time to understand. Demonstrating that you understand can be strong medicine for a distraught client.

2. It prevents you from jumping in with a question and thus closing down or redirecting your client's thought development. It is akin to nonjudgmental, non-directive grunts, silences, and comments such as "I see," "Tell me more," and "Go ahead."

3. It builds rapport. It is overwhelming to be listened to: not replied to, not graded, not contradicted, not encouraged, just listened to, as if, banish the thought, you had something interesting to say.

4. It gets you off the hot seat. You may panic when a client asks, "How will I take care of the kids?" Yours is not to solve this problem but rather to help the client think it though. "You are concerned about the children." Responsibility stays on the other side of the desk.

Practice. Ask a friend to spend 15 minutes describing a family, school, or work problem. When the person pauses, just reflect back what was said. Don't offer judgment ("I agree with that"); don't ask specific questions ("What did he say then?"); don't shift the flow to your liking ("Oh, that's interesting. Tell me more about that."); and don't try to fix the problem. (You can't fix a problem until you confirm what it is, anyway). Just listen and reflect back.

"You are saying THIS about THAT?"

Restate what was said in your own words. Don't use an active listening response after every pause; otherwise, things get awkward and the speaker will soon resent what you are doing. Throw in an occasional "I see" or supportive grunt.

You will feel a little bit stupid doing this. But once you get the knack of it, it will become more natural and feel less artificial. "Your saying that active listening will become easier and more authentic?"

Yes, that's what we are saying. Of course, it can be overdone. A cartoon shows a patient shouting at his psychiatrist, "Yes, I said for some reason people don't seem to like me. Open your ears, fat-head!"

Next Steps

After the interview, tell your client exactly what you are going to do next and what you expect them to do. Put it in writing, if you can, in a followup communication. Then do it. Then promptly tell them you did it when you did it.

1. If you do what you say you are going to do, your clients will trust you and you will sleep better.

2. If you tell them what you did your clients will appreciate you. The number one bar complaint from clients is *"My lawyer won't tell me what is going on."*

We know of one lawyer who advertised in the yellow pages with a simple: *"We return all your phone calls promptly."* Her business boomed. (A student once told us that he was so afraid of the Socratic Method that he would have gone to any school that said "We don't use it." You never know what sells.)

COUNSELING

Helping Clients Decide

Your job is to help your clients think through and then evaluate their options. This is true *even when* the client has already made up his mind. Probing on your part ("Why do you think that's a good idea?") may disclose that the decision rests on inaccurate information, inflated optimism, or fails to account for important matters.

"Sure, we can sue the bastard. He deserves it. But litigation is a horrible thing to go through. It may take years and may become the most consuming thing in your life."

"Macbeth, the witches have been wrong before."

List making helps.

If we decide to do A, what will be the:

—Best outcome?

—Worst outcome?

—Most likely outcome?

If we decide not to do A, what will be the:

—Best outcome?

—Worst outcome?

—Most likely outcome?

Clarifying goals helps, too. Clients often need help identifying what is really important to them. *I want security for my family. I want more time with the kids. I want to be vindicated.* (Watch out for that one. Vindication is elusive.) Clear goals narrow the options and shorten the list.

Time frames are important. Consider both the short-term and long-term implications of the decision. Pushing a competitor to the wall might be good for short term profits but not for long term relationships.

We often focus on the legal and economic dimensions of a decision, overlooking the psychological and the societal.

If we settle, how will you feel about your decision? Will you feel vindicated or that you sold out? How will you feel about it in a couple of years?

How will it impact on your family? What kind of message are you sending?

Of course decisions do not turn on lists, on adding up the pros and cons. Often we go with the shorter list and we have all flipped a coin when we can't make up our minds, only to insist we go two out of three when it comes up heads. Lists inform the irrational part of our mind of factors it should mull over.

Too much information, too much list making and mulling over, can get in the way of good decisions—they can paralyze and confuse. We can hold only so much information. To improve the ability of doctors to diagnose heart attacks, a Chicago hospital simplified the decision by making less information available—diagnoses improved.

Have a Plan B

You have given your client accurate information and explained the law clearly. But your client still thinks that the Cow can clear the Moon on the first jump while your professional judgment is screaming "*splat!*". It's time to help your client create Plan B. The earlier the better for Plan B—long before the Cow gathers speed on the runway. You don't want to start thinking about Plan B in crisis mode.

What would you do?

Was a time when doctors and lawyers told you what to do; they knew best. Once the Wisconsin State Bar Journal advised: *The client will feel better and more secure if told what to do and how to do it, without an explanation of how you reached your conclusions.* Today that would be dismissed as quaint and elitist; today we stress personal autonomy, replete with a long list of side effects.

There is a lot to be said for having clients decide. It is their life, after all, and we all value the factors at play ("freedom," "face" and "money"), differently. Further it is empowering to make one's own decision and, it is always nice, if things go south, to point out, "Well, it was your decision."

Professional passivity, however, has its limits. Clients don't always know best: they can make horrible decisions resting on misunderstandings facts or stemming from wild expectations. While it's their life, the problem is that it's their life. They can only see trees where you can step back and see the forest. Good counselors confront and push.

Refusing to say what you would do has other problems. It may leave the client feeling isolated. Eight thousand patients at a Chicago hospital were interviewed. All wanted to know their options and wanted the doctors to consider their opinion; two thirds wanted the doctors to decide. There are differences of course but one physician said that patients want their doctors "to be standing in the circle with them."

If you have a strong opinion as to what the client should decide you may unconsciously manipulate the facts so as to compel that decision. It has been said that if someone believes they are standing on a cliff they will not step over unless they intend suicide. In discussing pro and cons you may be painting a cliff. Maybe it is better just to be up front with your opinion.

Telling your client what you would do is not the end of the matter. It becomes just another factor for the client to consider, the ultimate decision always rests with the client. As Sartre once said, even if God came down to tell you what to do, you would still have to decide whether it was God or the Devil in disguise.

To give neutral advice realize *you have a dog in the fight.* Maybe it's your desire to get the matter closed, maybe it's your desire to go to trial, or maybe it's your desire to impress a supervisor. The problem is acute in the "repeat player" situation—where, as in most practices, you will face the same opponent time and time again. Do you want to make nice or do you want to make mean?

Some Decisions are Yours

Whether to settle, plea or waive a jury trial are decisions that belong to your client. Clients set the goals. Whether to object, file a motion or call Wicked Uncle Ernie to testify are decisions that belong to you. You should consult with your clients, for sure, but "how to get there" decisions are why they will pay you the big bucks.

When Good Clients Go Bad: Paving Paradise

You are in very hot water if you assist a client in committing a fraud or a crime (and it is no defense that a senior partner ordered you to or that the guy down the block would have done it if you hadn't). But what if your client plans to do something that, while legal, is repulsive, like pave paradise and put in a parking lot?

(Some might not find this repulsive—what with advent of the Law and Economics Movement, it is becoming increasing difficult to think of something all would agree is repulsive.)

It is perfectly OK to withdraw from your representation unless you are involved in actual litigation and there things get stickier. Short of withdrawal can you say "That sucks"? Not only can you but you should.

As a good counselor you must help the client think through aspects of the decision that perhaps have not come to mind. Decisions might have moral, political, and even psychological dimensions. If you think something sucks, most likely others will as well: regulators, prosecutors, competitors, family members, and even the public. And stress the long term—the decision might come back in the middle of a dark and restless night, like the Ghost of Christmas Past.

An experienced lawyer came to a law class and was asked a law school favorite. You represent an insurance company and your doctor has examined the plaintiff and has found an aneurism which may kill him. The aneurism may have been caused by the accident thus increasing recoverable damages. The plaintiff is unaware of his condition. What do you do?

"Phone the plaintiff's lawyer and tell him."

"But your client, the insurance company. It might fire you?"

"I can always get another client."

"But isn't that covered by work product? Maybe you would be disbarred."

"I can always get other work."

INVESTIGATION: BE SKEPTICAL

Understanding what your client wants and understanding the law

As the King of Hearts told Alice: "*Begin at the beginning*," It is never a bad idea to triple check to make sure you on the same page as your client. And a quick look at the law will help you figure out what you want to look for. If your client's mother left all her money to the Cheshire Cat, it is good to know the law of competency before you talk to the butler and the hairdresser.

In addition to lay and expert witnesses, you can introduce *documents, physical evidence* and *demonstrative evidence.*

Visiting the Scene and Taking Photographs

A visit is worth a thousand interviews. A visit will often give you a real sense of what the witnesses saw and couldn't see and, in many cases, what your client went through.

Pictures help. To admit photos someone must testify that the photo is a "fair and accurate" representation (as opposed to, say, one that is "fair and balanced"). As the lawyer you can't testify as that would put your credibility at issue. You'll need someone else. If the size of the item is unclear include something of known size, a pencil or a dinosaur.

Who can you interview?

Everyone is fair game except *parties* to the lawsuit (unless opposing counsel grants permission). If a corporation is involved, are its *employees* parties? Some are; it depends on the jurisdiction. Generally the higher they are on the food chain the more likely they are parties. You can, of course, *depose* adverse parties. In some states Victim Rights Legislation places restrictions on defense lawyers interviewing victims (but not other witnesses). In some states you can *depose* represented parties even before filing a lawsuit.

Can you interview a *potential* adverse party who is unrepresented by counsel? There is no ethical rule that says you can't but be sensitive to allegations that you bullied or overreached. Probably it is best is to send a letter that lays out the beef. *Don't* purport to give the person legal advice ("The law requires you to do X"—at most "*Our position* is that the law requires you to do X.") Realize that the rest of the world is not accustomed to our "in-your-face, take no prisoners" writing style. "If you don't do X, which is very reasonable, we will be forced, quite reluctantly, to drop the Big One."

Your goals

1. *Figure out what you don't know and where you might find it.*

Do a little preliminary sleuthing. Lots of information is sitting out there waiting for you to get your hands on it. Public records, police reports are all accessible. The internet is magical. The person you want to sue may have a non-private Facebook page. Caveat: You can't introduce that Wikipedia page into evidence; you still need to track down those witnesses and documents.

2. *Find out what the witness knows and the basis of that knowledge.*

What is the foundation of the knowledge—observation, hearsay, speculation, a newspaper story, or fond hopes? How would you cross-examine the witness? Even hostile witnesses can know things that will help your case. Before you talk to that witness clearly state who you are and who you represent.

3. *Find out what the witness doesn't know.*

"Do you know anything else?" "So you didn't see the accident itself."

4. *Find additional leads.*

Hearsay and speculation are fine. Does the witness know other witnesses? Know of any documents? Of smoking guns?

5. *Pursue the bad stuff.*

Hearing something harmful to your case you'll want to duck, to hope that it will disappear. It won't. You'll meet it again at trial or during negotiation. Time to prepare is now.

6. *There are limits to what you can say to witnesses.*

Advise your *client* not to talk to anyone. But you can't request other witnesses not to talk to another party. You can't give them any legal advice at all—except to advise them that they may need a lawyer.

Interview asap, memories fade and testimony can be corrupted talking to others and watching TV news stories. Because interviews with hostile witnesses need to be more focused, wait until you have a good idea of your case. *Make an immediate memorandum of your conversation—better yet, record your conversation. Your memory will fade.*

Reluctant witnesses

"I don't want to get involved. I'm busy. I hate your client."

Never lie. Tell them you are a lawyer and who you represent. *Never* ask "Will you talk with me?" Used car salespeople *never* ask if you want to buy the car. Rather, they project the belief that you will. Writing up the contract ("Just to see how it looks on paper"), they ask you to sign so they can see if they can get the "super deal" past the manager. You become convinced that you have already agreed to buy the car; it's just that you can't remember when. To say "No" at this point would be like breaking your promise.

It is much easier *to refuse to begin* a conversation than it is *to end it.* Get the witness talking. Make small talk before moving to threatening material. If the person refuses to talk with you, shift from confrontation to explanation; ask the witness why. Don't increase reluctance by taking notes. Take out the yellow pad (or tape recorder) only after the interview is going well, "Just to make sure I get it all right."

While you can't guarantee the witness that they will not be involved in a trial, you can point out that most cases settle and their cooperation at this stage will make that more likely. In civil matters, if all else fails, you can threaten to take their deposition.

Getting the Truth

We've read some police manuals but they don't help much. Police have better leverage.

How can you tell if a witness is lying? One way is to ask a series of nonthreatening questions and watch the facial expressions and body language. When you ask the key question, do these change? This, of course, has absolutely no evidentiary value.

Warding off lies may be easier. "I've been to the scene and from where you say you were standing it would be impossible to see the color of the light. Right?" Another device is to convince the person you know the truth and are only confirming details.

"Others have told me the whole story, I just want to confirm some details."

Or you can say something outrageous, forcing the source to correct it and, while doing so, reveal what you are really trying to find out.

Where to Interview and Interviewing by Phone

Where do you want to interview the witness? Should you write a letter or call the witness to set things up? Or is it better to show up unannounced?

Be solicitous of neutral and friendly witnesses as they can make or break your case. As to hostile witnesses, commentators generally advise showing up at their homes or work, unannounced, the theory being that they will generally not agree to an appointment and that surprise prevents them from getting "steeled." On the other hand, hostility generated now may come back to bite you at trial. In this game, everyone is a repeat player.

It is common to do some investigation by telephone. First, do not record the conversation unless you tell the other person. Second, consider a follow-up letter to the other party embodying what was said and asking if your understanding of the conversation is correct. Third, note all telephone calls in the case file with a brief description of what was said. Fourth, if the person at the other end does not believe you are a lawyer, refer him to your website or offer to explain "per stirpes."

From an evidentiary standpoint, what you get by telephone is fairly worthless. You will not be able to testify as to what was said and, if an investigator made the call, there may be problems with authenticating that the person on the other end was the person the investigator thought.

Write up the Interview

Having told you one thing in an interview it is unlikely that the witness will look you in the eye during trial and change his story. If he does, that's a problem. As the lawyer in the case you cannot prove up the inconsistent statement as it puts your credibility at issue. You can avoid this problem by having a third party at the interview or by having the witness sign the statement.

The value of a signed statement goes well beyond this. Signed witness statements help during negotiations. And, of course, when you write them up you will see all you forgot to ask.

Darn.

TAKING AND DEFENDING DEPOSITIONS

Discovery is boring. That's our basic insight. The rest is filler.

Sit in on a few. Books and seminars are like candy, dandy. However you need to see for yourself. How does the questioner introduce the process? How do the lawyers handle objections? Is it as boring as we think?

Taking a Deposition

Basic choices

Why a Deposition? Why not just an interview? It's cheaper and your opponent isn't sitting in the room learning what the witness has to say and something of your case. Formal discovery, however, has several advantages: you can depose the adverse parties (you can't interview them); you can *subpoena* both reluctant witnesses and documents; answers are under *oath*; and you'll have a *transcript*—it is hard to impeach a witness with prior statements made informally. Depose, for sure, key witnesses who might not be there for trial.

Early or Late? Getting the jump pays. Your opponent realizes that you are serious and that the litigation is going to be expensive. Settlement looks better. An early deposition commits your opponent to a version of the facts and gives you time to explore leads and check the dubious aspects of your opponent's yarn. But there is always something to be said for the turtle: the more you know before you take a deposition, the more effective you will be in focusing the inquiry.

Who's on First? At trial generally you call your client *after* your other witnesses to prevent your adversary from establishing inconsistencies between what your client said and what your witnesses say. Turn this ploy around; depose the adverse party *before* you depose the henchmen. For the same reason best to depose the adverse party *before* your opponent deposes your client.

Interrogatories Before Depositions? Interrogatories are cheap and will clear up the basics allowing for a better and more focused deposition. Federal rules limit the number of interrogatories and this may be a factor to consider. Serving interrogatories will force the opposing lawyer to meet with the client to discuss the case—lazy lawyers often don't; no need to trigger good lawyering. Further, answering interrogatories, your opponent will be learning about your case and the deposition testimony may be tailored in light of this knowledge.

Bring Your Client? Generally yes unless there will be emotional issues. Your client can help you with follow-up questions, and to deter, by mere presence, exaggerations and perjury. Having your client see the other side's evidence may also spur settlement—you won't have to *explain,* "This guy's gonna kill you."

What Can You Ask?

You should review your state statutes on discovery. Are there any prohibited topics, such as privilege and work-product? Must you restrict yourself to seeking admissible evidence?

Under the federal rules, you can't ask about privileged matter (what the client and lawyer talked about) but other than that you can ask about any relevant evidence with relevant being defined as appearing *"reasonably calculated to lead to the discovery of admissible evidence."* So you can pursue hearsay and speculation.

Confront the witness?

The witness says contradictory things, makes statements inconsistent with a prior statement, or swears to something that is easily refutable by a document you have in your file. Should you seek blood? Difficult issue.

If you confront the witness, even if he can't think of an explanation just then, by the time trial rolls around, expect a very fine one. On the other hand, if you save the confrontation for trial, there is always the chance that the witness has a good explanation, and you will look rather silly. Further, by waiting, you will not have time to check the truth of the explanation. If your attack succeeds your opponent might rethink the case and settle. That said, most advise to save impeachment for trial. However *definitely* confront the witness if it is likely that the witness will not testify at trial and the deposition will be introduced. Double check the rules of evidence in your state on unavailable witnesses.

Dealing with objections

There is a critical distinction between your opponent *objecting* to your questions and your opponent *instructing* the witness not to answer.

Your question: Tell me your impressions of what was going on after the accident.

Opponent: Objection. Calls for speculation, calls for narrative, and lack of foundation.

The ball is now in your court. You can rephrase the question *or* you can tell the witness, "Go ahead and answer." If you are interested in using the answer at trial, *rephrase the question.* If you don't, your opponent can object at trial and, if sustained, the answer won't come in. On the other hand, if you don't care about using the answer, tell the witness to answer the question.

Your question: Tell me your impressions of what was going on after the accident.

Opponent: Objection. Calls for speculation, calls for narrative, and lack of foundation.

You: Objection noted. Go ahead and answer the question.

Now the ball is back in your opponent's court. She can give up *or* instruct the witness not to answer the question. The latter is risky. Under the federal rules, the *only time* your opponent can *instruct* a witness not to answer is to protect a privilege, enforce a prior court sanctioned limitation, or to bring a motion to the effect that you are conducting the deposition in bad faith or are unreasonably abusing the witness. So says Rule 30.

Dealing with Jerks

Obnoxious litigators, smelling blood, will try to scare you into early retirement. Unwarranted objections, speaking clarifications, and shameless uncivility are the weapons. If you know your stuff, not to worry. The federal rules provide:

Any objection during a deposition must be stated concisely and in a non-argumentative and non-suggestive manner. Rule 30.

Remain calm and focused. Video cameras work wonders. Put the problem on the record.

"Let me stop for a moment right here. You have made several unwarranted objections and have repeatedly interrupted me. If you don't stop this disruptive behavior, I will adjourn the deposition, go to court and seek sanctions."

If the behavior continues, follow through: seek sanctions. Realize yet again that *you* are on trial: establish that you will not suffer fools.

Preparing for Impeachment

"Yes, I did say that during the deposition. But I was sick and my meds confused me. I didn't understand your question and my answer was just a wild guess anyway. Besides, it was a bad hair day."

An opening riff will help.

"Before we begin, are you feeling OK? On any medication? Don't answer my question unless you understand it and don't guess. Your hair looks great but how are you in terms of existential angst?"

Your goals are pretty much the same as those we discussed in our chapter on witness interviewing. Commit the witness to specifics, one at a time. (That's why it's so boring.)

Defending a deposition

Prepare thy self and thy witness

Spend serious time preparing the deposition *you* would take. This will provide a ground upon which your opponent's thinking will jump out. What was your opponent's goal in exploring areas you did not anticipate? Why didn't your opponent explore areas you would have?

Lawyers never allow their clients to testify at *trial* unprepared yet many have their witnesses simply *show up* for their deposition. Big mistake. Most cases settle, and a major factor on the settlement is how well the client and witnesses do during their depositions.

Warn your witness not to guess. "I don't know" is a legitimate response to a deposition question (unlike that in an interrogatory where there is a duty to investigate). *Just answer the question and don't volunteer.* That's fine, but the witness may still want to volunteer. As The Animals sang: "*Oh Lord, please don't let me be misunderstood.*" People are dying to explain themselves.

"You'll want to volunteer information to tell your side of the story. Don't. There is no way you are going to convince the other lawyer you are in the right. And the lawyer will likely be friendly, but the lawyer is not your friend. The lawyer is being paid to go after you."

They can tell their side at trial. Tell them it is fine if asked to admit to "inconvenient facts," and warn them that trying to explain them away just makes things worse. *Pause and think before answering*. While long pauses look bad at trial, they will not show on a written transcript.

Making Objections

Leave hearsay, speculation, and irrelevant at home. You can make these objections at trial if the answer is being offered as evidence. You do wave "lack of foundation" and most objections based on the form of the question, the theory being is that your opponent can then remedy the problem. But that you can make an objection does not mean you should make an objection. Often it simply allows your opponent to ask clearer questions and lay more adequate foundations.

Be leery, however, of vague questions:

> *Q: Is there anything else I should know?*
>
> *Q: Is there anything else you would like to add?*

The fear is that the witness may volunteer harmful information. While your opponent is entitled to develop harmful information, insist that it be disclosed only by focused questions. Also be leery of questions that attempt to commit the witness to specific estimates of such things as time, distance and speed.

If the question seeks privileged material instruct the witness not to answer.

Asking Questions

At the end of the deposition, you can question the witness. Generally don't.

You might want to question the witness if you think it would be important in settlement negotiations. Realizing that the transcript might be the only thing higher ups review in terms of settlement, you might want bring in a few strong points.

Should you clear up misstatements? You must; the question is when. Two dangers: you underline the significance of the misstatement and might make things worse. In a few weeks you will get a copy of the transcript for the witness to sign. Have the witness read and sign. You can add an addendum with additions, qualifications, and corrections.

"On page 18, as to the question concerning the meaning of life, I was confused. Upon reflection, my answer is that the unexamined life is worth living, in fact, it's a whole lot better."

Back at the office

Whether you took or defended the deposition, when you get back to the office write a memo addressing two questions:

1. What did my *opponent* learn of *my* case?

2. What did *I* learn about my *opponent's* case?

Defending, it's mostly sitting there

A minister sees God sitting in the first pew. He phones the Bishop who is skeptical and advises a vacation. The minister insists and eventually the Bishop agrees to come to see for himself. There, in the first pew, sits God.

"Over there," whispers the minister. "I see," replies the Bishop.

"What should we do?"

"Look busy."

NEGOTIATION

Goals, BATNA, and Collateral Issues

Don't go in to "test the waters" or to "see what they have in mind." Know what you want. Better yet, know what your client wants. Clarity is critical. Negotiating a settlement that your client doesn't want won't make your day better. *"I told you that it was a deal breaker that I get the Vegematic".*

Consider *writing* out a complete settlement agreement, something you would be happy to live with but also something you think your opposite could live with. There is not much point trying to convince the other side to agree to something they'll never agree to. Are there ways of making you both happy?

Another key piece of planning is BATNA: *Best Alternative to Negotiated Agreement.* What are your client's alternatives if agreement is not reached, and how costly will they be? This will give you a sense of when to walk out. Consider the controversy from the opposition's viewpoint. What might its goals be? What problems might it face? What will it risk from stalemate? What is its BATNA?

In evaluating your case, consider collateral factors:

Avoiding risk and delay

Vindicating important principles

Saving face

Creating good, or avoiding bad, precedent

Looking good to significant others

These concerns impact not only your opponent but also your opponent's lawyer, not only your client, but *you*. Often they can become part of the negotiation—an apology, a promise not to brag, the assurance "You did a great job for your client."

Listen, probe, and deflect

Listen, not to respond, not to find fault, but simply to understand the other's position or learn something you did not yet know. You may suddenly realize that there is a lot you can come together on. You may find common ground or a way to meet their needs at little cost to your client. Or you may learn that your case or perhaps your opponent's isn't as strong as you thought.

Probe:

"Why do you think that is a fair proposal?"

"Why don't you think your client will agree to mine?"

Avoid jumping in to contest. There is a sense if we don't immediately take issue with an opponent's point we concede it.

"Not so fast there. That argument simply ignores . . . . "

"Stop right there. That simply isn't true."

You can keep your opponent talking without acknowledging the validity of what's being said. Practice deflections.

"I don't necessarily agree with that, but keep going."

"I'm listening."

"We'll get back to that but tell me more."

Deflecting gracefully is a skill worth developing, far better than lying.

"So just how badly does you client want this deal?"

Our first impulse is to lie—"Not much at all. Scores of other opportunities." But this leads to bad reputations and unethical behavior Deflect:

"That's not the issue. Let's get back to our prior discussion."

"Good question. But first let's discuss . . . "

"Come on, I'm not going to answer that kind of question."

We were brought up to be polite—get over it. Just because someone asks you a question doesn't mean you have to answer it.

Playing Hardball or Solving Problems?

Hardball views negotiation as a game to be *won*. The two parties stake out initial positions and slowly come together on a solution. ("I will be back by midnight." "No, you get home by 9.") It is marked by zero-sum thinking (what I get, you lose), puffing one's position while attacking the opposition, and keeping secrets while gathering "intelligence." A typical hardball ploy is a very high demand (or very low offer), followed by small and painful concessions, accompanied with threats of walkout.

Problem-solving views conflicts as problems to be solved. It *rejects* zero-sum thinking: pies can be expanded, not just divided. It *rejects* secrecy: needs and goals are to be shared in search of a better resolution. Lawyers make lists not threats.

Problem-solving has substantial benefits. Hardball will *not* produce the best agreement for *both* parties: it conceals and frequently misstates information. Ideal solutions, again from the perspectives of *both* parties, simply *cannot* be reached under these circumstances. Still most of us are reluctant to be too open, fearing that if we share our wishes our opponent will exploit them, turning our needs into our vulnerabilities.

Most negotiations are a mixture of the styles. Your approach will depend on who you are (Are you trustful? Do you enjoy high stakes poker?), on how much you trust your opponent, and on the kind of negotiation you are involved with (problem solving is best when you are dealing with parties who will have long-term relationships, where good solutions for *both* parties are paramount). The good news is that studies have shown that both kinds of negotiators can be quite effective.

First and Initial Offers

We *fear* that we have grossly miscalculated and we *hope* that our opponent has. If the other side goes first, we won't be stuck with our ill-conceived offer, and we may get one that is better than our wildest dream. However, the more experienced the lawyers are, the less likely either has miscalculated. Realize that letting your opponent go first has a definite cost. The first offer becomes the base—you will have to *force* concessions rather than be convinced to *make* concessions.

Once you decide whether you want to go first or second, think about how you can make this happen. How can you trigger their first response, how can you deflect their insistence "After you"?

"Splitting the difference" is traditional and may lead to extreme initial positions. But if you come in too high or too low you put no pressure on your opponent to settle. Your initial position should be reasonable in the sense that you can defend it as being fair. All of that said, convention dictates that you build in some fat, dollars or issues, for trading purposes. You will want to leave your opponents with the sense that they "got something." A total rout on your part bodes ill for future relationships.

Some lawyers make an extremely high or low offer just to test the waters, just to see your reaction. Rather than making a counteroffer, consider simply rejecting the offer outright and refuse to say why. Saying why discloses something of your position.

> *"I reject that offer and I'm not making a counteroffer. If you want to continue the negotiation, make a better one."*

Keeping Secrets

There are three kinds of matters that you might want to keep secret: your client's needs, your trial evidence, and your eagerness to settle. Let's take them in reverse order.

Don't disclose your *eagerness* to settle. When a couple is dating, the one who is less committed to the relationship gets to pick the movie. As to *evidence*, should you save the ace of trumps to spring at trial? Disclose it and your opponent can prepare. Generally, however, it is a bad idea to hold back. To convince your opponent of the strength of your case, holding back key evidence won't help. Besides, with discovery, secrets are very hard to keep. Some personal injury lawyers prepare *settlement brochures* which lay out the claims and theories in great detail.

Finally, the difficult issue of *needs*. In hardball negotiation, never disclose. A problem-solving approach would be less dogmatic. It generally favors disclosure of needs as that leads to better settlements and more satisfied participants. Secrecy is the enemy of problem-solving. If both sides are committed to the approach, if both are trustworthy, then disclosure works. How do you know your opponent is committed? Hammer out ground rules before you begin:

> *"We will take turns disclosing our clients' interests, needs and goals, and agree not to exploit them by changing demands in light of the disclosed material."*

> *"When we make proposals, we will disclose how they help meet the needs of our clients and will justify them in terms of fairness rather than by the threat of deadlock."*

Making Concessions

Make one concession and the next thing you know your opponent demands Omaha. To avoid the appearance of rout, *give reasons* for your concessions. Don't just come down $8,000. "If we settle now, we'll save about that amount in attorney's fees." "Just to get the ball rolling, I will consider dropping the demand by that amount." It helps to ask your opponent just why it is fair to cut

$8,000 from your claim. If the reason is a good one, use it to justify your concession. Another graceful way to make concessions is to *link* them. "I will come down $8,000 *if* you agree to call your dog off."

Be aware of "Once I got it, I don't want it." If you concede Omaha too quickly, your opponent may value it less. "Maybe they know something about Omaha I don't. Maybe it isn't the hog butcher for the world. Maybe it's Chicago."

Making Threats and Avoiding Deadlock

A creditable "last offer" on your part engenders tremendous psychological pressure. Accept it or stalemate. Stalemate, with all its traumas and uncertainties, becomes your opponent's responsibility. Acceptance, on the other hand, means certainty, finality and, of course, no more work.

But how to make your threat creditable? The philosopher Robert Nozick defined the perfect philosophical argument as one which, if rejected, sets up vibrations in the mind of the naysayer that slowly, but surely, kill. We don't have a "Nozick Pill."

To make your threat believable, *mean it.* Don't make "last offers" as a puffing device. If you and your client are clear on your *stalemate position*, then meaning it won't be a problem. "We feel that further concessions make us worse off than not settling."

Second, take *steps.* If you are really willing to break off negotiations, what would you do? Set depositions. Look for alternative suppliers.

What if you opponent begins painting herself in a corner before you can even get your brushes out?

Change the offer by adding, deleting or rewriting a term. This will force your opponent to reassess and come, once again, to the painful decision to risk deadlock. *Change the players.* Perhaps the problem is with personalities. Ask the other lawyer if there is someone else that could step in or if there is someone else in the corporation that should be involved. Consider stepping aside yourself.

Avoiding Nasty Ploys

The Used Car Dealer. Once it seems you have an agreement, your opponent claims to lack authority to settle and has to run the deal by the client or supervisor. Guess what? If you suspect your opponent might do this, before you get underway, ask *"Do you have authority to settle this right now?"*

A related ploy is to spring an additional demand at the last minute, hoping that, having come this far, you will be likely to give in. Smoke out this ploy: "Before I give you my reaction to this proposal, I want to know if there are other matters it does not include?"

Some negotiators engage in subtle irritants, being late, mispronouncing your name. Oh well.

Avoiding Misunderstanding and Keeping Your Good Name

Put aside style and technique, the most important factor is your reputation for honesty and for keeping your word. Don't lie and keep your promises. But it takes more than that.

"You promised X."

"No I didn't. Maybe you thought I did but I really didn't."

"That's a lie."

In the heat of negotiation both sides hear what they want to hear and often misinterpret what was said. Make sure your adversary understands that you are "considering" X but not promising X. If you think there may be misunderstandings send a follow up letter or simply pause periodically during the negotiation to review exactly what was agreed to and what has not.

Negotiation by Mail

Negotiating by mail invites a considered response, a response that is often difficult in face-to-face negotiations. During a face-to-face negotiation, when you make a point, likely your adversary will deny it just to keep the matter open because it seems that *unless it is denied, it is admitted.* Knee-jerk "nots" lead to stalemate. Having your arguments in written form, your adversary will have time to consider them without immediately reacting to them.

Write the Agreement

There will be gaps and ambiguities in what was hashed out. Without violating the spirit of the agreement, you can fill omissions and resolve ambiguities so as to protect your client. Because you are writing it from the perspective of your client, you will see omissions that your opponent probably would not.

The downside is the rule of interpretation which holds that, in the event of ambiguity, agreements are read against the drafter. This rule makes sense; given the psychological viewpoint, the drafter should be more sensitive to ambiguities that go against him.

If you are settling a case that would otherwise be litigated, be *sure* to cover what happens if the other side refuses to carry out the settlement. *Are you stuck with a suit on the settlement or can you reinstate the main lawsuit*?

No Gloating

Never, even if it feels right. Always congratulate your opponents on how tough they were, what a good deal they got, and, as to credit, give them the lion's share.

The easiest thing to give up is credit. That was Gary Bellow's advice.

MAKING DEALS

"Doers" *do*; lawyers *caution*.

Folks embarking on a new relationship are usually optimistic and part of your job is to be the bearer of *possible,* but not of *certain,* bad news. We graduate from law school as Eeyores, viewing a world where all contracts are broken and all practical jokes lead to intensive care.

Essential topics

1. *Duties*: Who is to do what, when, and for what price?

2. *Contingencies*: What effect will they have on respective duties?

3. *Failures and disputes*: What happens if one side doesn't perform?

4. *Enforceability:* Do the parties want to be legally bound?

Here are some questions you might ask your *client*:

Do you want a legally enforceable deal?

Often parties want a framework for future cooperation but do not want to make legally enforceable deal. You might want to explain some of the pros and cons, such things as the possibility of receiving, or paying, damages and injunctive relief. While we all want to commit the other side and maintain total freedom ourselves, the mutuality doctrine may make the contract unenforceable. Even if we bind ourselves only to "good faith," that can come back to bite us in suits alleging bad faith.

What will you do if an agreement isn't reached?

Knowledge of alternatives greatly strengthens your bargaining position. They will suggest the point at which to walk away from negotiations and will bring clarity about the objectives.

What do you want to accomplish?

Usually the trade-offs are price, quality, service, and warranties. But other things may matter to your client: timing, control, world peace, or Corinthian leather.

What can go wrong?

"It's two years from now. What could have gone wrong?" Increased costs? Strikes? Acquisitions? Pro wrestling discovered to be real? As we will see, it is not necessary to cover every contingency in the agreement but there is no excuse to *assume* that the world will forever stay the same.

How should disputes be resolved?

A lot of creative work is being done in the area of dispute resolution: terms requiring cooling off periods, mediation or arbitration. All of these deserve a serious look. Consider carefully, however, the interplay of the formal and informal methods of dispute resolution. In many enterprises there is a strong tradition of informal dispute resolution, *i.e.* the telephone. If the parties can't work it out perhaps quick termination and litigation are appropriate, rather than forcing them to stay together by requiring additional hurdles such as mediation.

Form books and *checklists* will be quite helpful. Reading a form contract focus on each term, "Do I need something like that?" Don't include things simply because someone else did. It is very *difficult to see what's not there*. Before consulting form books, list everything you think the agreement should cover.

Early on draft an agreement that your client would be happy with. Even if you never show it to the other side, writing it will do wonders to help you think things through.

Contingencies

Say that the deal will be affected if pro wrestling is found to be real. (This gets boring for us as well). If you bring the contingency up:

1. *Maybe the other party will agree to assume the risk;*

2. *Maybe your client will be forced to assume the risk; or*

3. *Maybe the negotiations will deadlock (over an event that is unlikely to occur)* .

If neither side wants to assume the risk, you might be able to avoid deadlock by kicking the can down the road (a now famous political expression) by providing that the issue, if it arises, will be resolved by "good faith" negotiations or arbitration.

What if the agreement is silent as to the contingency? If it doesn't arise, nothing. If it does arise, the world does not end. The parties either will work it out or go to court. Note that at that time the parties will have more information and their agreement *then* might make more sense than their agreement *now.*

Bring up matters that may go bump in the night and let your client decide how to handle them during negotiation. However, if a client is taking a foolish risk by insisting that you not raise a contingency during negotiations, write a letter to the client indicating that you advised as to the risk.

Precision

The *promise* of precise drafting (replete with definitions and subparts) is that it limits discretion; the *problem* with precise drafting (other than boring, pedantic and costly) is that it limits discretion.

> *Early statutes defined "theft" as a "felonious taking." What did that mean? Reformers were uncomfortable (they always are). Redrafted, theft became "to take an object of value with the intent to deprive the owner of said object permanently." In the old days, mothers who stole food for starving babies walked free: whatever a "felonious taking" was, that wasn't it. But it was permanently depriving the owner of valuable bread.*

Precision may be the enemy of compromise. In China, around the time of Confucius, there was a debate about whether the laws should be written down. The argument *against* this was that once the law was written, people would insist upon their rights, whereas in a just society people compromise. Vagueness encourages compromise and vagueness allows for flexibility.

We are not advocating sloppiness. But realize the costs of lengthy documents, drafted with precision. Perhaps you better serve your client with a (cheap) short memorandum of understanding that will allow for compromise down the road. However if there are key points which will likely be disputed ("Do holidays include Columbus day?")—clean them up.

Uninvited guests

Will third parties benefit or be harmed by the agreement? Can third parties base claims on "third party beneficiary" or negligence analysis? You can draft around "third party beneficiary" problems (but good luck on the negligence claims) by explicitly stating no such beneficiaries are intended.

Make sure you are not an uninvited guest. The potential disaster is the tort of interference with contract, third parties suing your client for entering into a contract with someone they had been dealing with. "*Are you dealing with other parties concerning this?*"

Problems of long negotiations

If you are engaged in lengthy negotiations and one of the parties is spending considerable time and funds in the expectation that an agreement will be reached, beware! Agree, early on, who pays for these preparations if the deal falls though.

Another potential problem is that during the course of long negotiations parties may come to agreements as to some issues but may give them up in light of further concessions. Drafting the final agreement, be sure that earlier agreements are either *included* or *explicitly excluded*. Use an *integration* clause.

Drafting Contracts of Adhesion

Warm zeal and the defense of the unpopular are our grandest traditions. But they were forged in the hot fire of the adversary system. There, every move is scrutinized by the opposition. But lawyers are often asked to draft agreements that will *not* be negotiated or scrutinized, but will be *imposed*: form sales contracts, form leases, and form software licenses.

As a legal matter, the more one-sided the agreement, the more likely it will be interpreted against you or thrown out as unconscionable or as against public policy. Woe to the client who, relying on your well-drafted exculpatory clause, failed to obtain liability insurance.

When there is no adversary, rethink your role. Be leery of buying your client's argument that his customers are deadbeats, anxious to sue in far off venues on bogus law suits. It is appropriate to share not only your legal opinion but also your moral opinion. And you can always refuse.

LEGAL WRITING

The fish are jumpin, And the cotton is high,
Oh, your daddy's rich, And your ma is good lookin,
So hush little baby, Don't you cry.

What a muddle! Sloppy work. Should baby hush *only if* the fish are jumpin, the cotton high, the daddy rich, *and* the ma good lookin. Or will one, say jumpin fish, do the trick? Put it to music. Might make more sense.

RILS Transitions

This is our most important advice: use effective transitions.

Next, let's talk jumpin fish.

This transition doesn't tell the reader what is its relationship to the prior topic, 'high cotton,' nor does it tell the reader just why we are talking about jumpin fish (it does introduce the topic, we'll give it that.) Compare:

For baby to hush, not only must the cotton be high, the fish must be jumpin.

This transition introduces the topic (jumpin fish), shows its legal relevance (hushing baby) and flags its relationship to 'high cotton.' *The relationship between elements is either an "and" or a "or."* As written, it shows an "and" relationship. Were it "or":

Even if the cotton is high isn't high, baby should still hush if the fish are jumpin.

We call these transitions "*RILS*": they Introduce the topic, the show its Relationship to the last topic and they tell the reader the Legal Significance of the topic. They not only help your reader they force you to back up to see how the tree fits in the forest.

Other than *RILS*, do we have any tips?

* *Quote, don't paraphrase; put law in context*

* *Be leery of Cut and Paste*

* *Don't force the reader to puzzle or go back*

* *Lead with your conclusions*

* *Be Explicit*

* *Ask "So what?"*

* *Murder your darlings*

Quote, don't paraphrase, and put the law in context

In the case of Riggs v. Palmer, it was held that no one shall be permitted to profit from his own wrong.

The reader has to take your word. Find *specific* language.

In the case of Riggs v. Palmer, it was held that "no one shall be permitted to profit from his own wrong."

Great. But what was the wrong? How was the person trying to profit? Citing a key case alert your reader to the context, not in great detail, but in broad strokes.

In the case of Riggs v. Palmer, it was held that 'No one shall be permitted to profit from his own wrong' (murderer denied inheriting his victim's estate).

A judge would want to know this before following precedent and denying a home builder his compensation because he double parked.

Beware cut and paste

Computer research is dandy but once you find your morsel (statutory or case language on point), don't cut and paste. *Copy the language yourself.* That's hard work and that's its virtue. You will read more carefully, copying only what you need. "Do I need that quote?" "Can I omit subpart B?" Copying discloses ambiguities and implications. "Wait a minute. I can interpret that word differently." Analyze *now*, not at a date to be named later.

Don't force your reader to go back or puzzle through

How many times have you been happily reading a case only to be abruptly stopped by: "The appellee argues. . . . " or "The same argument I made 20 pages ago applies here"? Have you ever gone back? Brief comments work wonders:

"The appellee (the plaintiff and the guy with the axe). . . ."

"The same argument I made 20 pages ago, to the effect that the world is flat, applies here."

Lead with your conclusions

The *goal of all legal writing* is to help someone (client, adversary, judge) come to a conclusion about an important matter. It is your job to give that person your best thinking. You are not Agatha Christie scattering clues (*x, y and z*) only to reveal that the butler did it. This forces the reader to go back, reviewing the clues to see if they really add up—"I don't even *remember* a butler!"

There should be no surprise endings in legal writing. They may work in jury argument but not in legal writing. Here your goal in writing is to simply to help someone make a difficult decision. Lead with your conclusion.

"My conclusion is that the butler did it because of x, y, and z."

Now readers can test and evaluate your conclusion as they go along: "Does *x* point to the butler?"

Be explicit

With Shakespearean flare, you write,

" Mark you well this: ma had been Ms. South Carolina."

While this is an interesting tidbit, but so what? Standing alone the reader is forced to tie the *specific fact* (her victory) to a *factual conclusion* (she's good lookin) and then tie the *factual conclusion* to its *legal significance* (baby should hush). Be nice.

Ma was Ms. South Carolina proving she's good lookin, so hush.

Sometimes your prose is implicit because you know too much. Having thought long and hard on the matter, it may be very clear to you how the fact (or legal point) fits in the legal analysis—realize your readers are first time players. On the other hand, implicitness might stem from your failure to think things through. Maybe you *don't* know how the fact (or legal point) fits in your legal analysis. Somehow it just seems important that she was Ms. South Carolina. Don't just put that down, ask *"So what?"* Tie your intuitions to your analysis.

Editing, as to every argument you make, as to every fact you cite, ask yourself "Can the first time player understand my point? Do I? So what?"

Can you be too explicit, seeming to be writing down to your reader? Sure, but not in legal writing.

Murder your darlings

On dark and stormy nights, novelists sweat blood and tears to compose compelling scenes, thrilling encounters, desperately trying to avoid the hackneyed opening. Then comes the cold, cruel light of morning and editing. "Yes, my love, my creation, you are quite brilliant, you dazzle, my best so far, but, alas, you don't fit."

In the trade it is known as "murdering your darlings." It ain't easy.

"Me? You're gonna delete me? You're kidding. You spent so much time, getting me just right. And you did! I'm the key to the whole thing; without me the center will not hold and things will fly apart. Look at that fat paragraph over there! Why, it's nothing but fluff. Cut it. Leave me. In fact, *expand me!*"

Editing

Let your draft sit a couple of days and then reread it *out loud.* You'll be surprised. As to each sentence, ask, "Do I have big words where shorter ones can do?" "Can I say this in fewer words?" "Can I make it more concrete?" "Can I make it more punchy?"

What follows are examples of bad writing and how to cure them.

Zap pretentious phrases:		
At the present time	*zap*	*now*
In the event	*zap*	*if*
In my considered opinion	*zap*	*I think*
Zap intensifiers, adjectives and adverbs:		
"It is very important to note"	*zap*	*"Note"* (or nothing at all)
"The lecture was boring."	*zap*	*"It put me to sleep."*
"The defendant lacked ethics."	*zap*	*"She stole $1,257,876.24."*
Zap passive verbs		
"The decision was reversed by the court."		*"The court reversed the decision."*
Zap verb derivatives:		
"Billy made a decision."		*"Billy decided."*

You are making your prose more spiffy, reducing clutter, and making it shorter. *Short is good.* (Short and happy even better). "Omit needless words," preached Strunk and White, the authors of the classic *Elements of Style*. Omitting needless words does not mean omitting detail or treating subjects in outline form. It means that *each word must tell.*

Your goal? Cutting 10%. Stephen King's first rejection slip read: *"Not bad, but puffy. You need to revise for length. Formula:*

2nd draft = 1st draft – 10%." If 10% works for him, it should work for us. 20% is even better.

Imagine the losing lawyer who received this decision from New York's highest court:

> *Although counsel candidly admits that his 284–page brief is unusually long, his claim that it is meticulously structured, thoroughly documented, exhaustively researched, carefully analyzed and comprehensively presented seems too self-congratulatory. His argument wanders aimlessly ... pausing only briefly to discuss the issues raised by this appeal ... This is in contrast to the brief filed on behalf of the Tax Commission which, even though consisting of only a 14–page argument on the merits, cogently and concisely discusses all of the issues presented* . Slater v. Galman, 38 NY 2d 1, 4 (1975)

Writing ain't easy

Writing is hard. A friend found James Joyce collapsed over his writing table.

> *"Is it the writing?"*
>
> *"It is always the writing."*
>
> *"How far did you get today?"*
>
> *"Nine words."*
>
> *"Nine words? That's not bad for you."*
>
> *"Yes. But I don't know the order they go in."*

Part Three
COURTROOM SKILLS

ORAL ARGUMENT

Forget Footnote 23 but not the facts

Oral argument is *different* than written argument. It's *not* the place to go over all of the arguments you made in your brief, including the one in footnote twenty-three which, admittedly, sparkles. In a brief cover all of your arguments; in oral argument *focus on the two or three that matter.* Go for the jugular!

The judges have already read your brief. Their eyes will glaze over if you begin to read it.

Precedent and policy are dandy but facts are critical. A good *statement of facts* puts the judges in your corner, looking at precedent and policy from your standpoint. Review what we said about telling stories. Briefly (1) tell the story from the perspective of your client, (2) have a spiffy opening, (3) avoid abstractions, adjectives, and blood oaths, (4) stress specific facts, (5) while acknowledging some inconvenient facts, don't make your opening one long apology, and (6) be honest.

Read your statement of facts to a ten year old and then ask, "Who is in the right?" If it's not your client, rewrite.

Be helpful and address the judges' concerns

This is serious business, not high school debate. Judges have heavy responsibilities; their decisions matter. This isn't about being smart, taking no prisoners, smoke and mirrors, or razzle-dazzle. Your job is to help the judges sort things out. You and your opponent are experts on the facts, on the law, and on the policy implications involved. Judges *need your help* in understanding the complexities, and they need to try out their reactions and to discuss their ideas. Rather than *argument,* think *conversation;* rather than *advocate*, think *teacher*.

Making an argument there are three possibilities:

1. The judges are *not* convinced and *never* will be; you are wasting your time.

2. The judges are *already* convinced; you are wasting your time.

3. The judges are *undecided* and *need* further guidance. In an ideal world you could simply stop and ask, "Well, Your Honors, have I convinced you on that one? If not, do I have a prayer?" But oral argument is highly stylized. How do you get these dragons out of their cave?

Give an overview of your arguments.

"I intend to argue the following three issues in this order. Would the court like me to address them in a different order? Or does it want me to address other issues?"

Maintaining eye contact, as opposed to reading your notes, allows you to gauge the judges' reactions.

Encourage Questions

Questions will enable you to address the judges' concerns *and* improve your performance. Lawyers are almost always better responding to questions than giving speeches. There is movement, creation, engagement. Some judges will pepper you with questions. Others are too shy to interrupt, too unsure to voice their concerns. How do you draw them out?

Want questions. Judges are people too, and human interaction is a subtle thing. If you fear questions, likely you won't get many. If you rejoice in them, they will come.

Don't assume questions are hostile. Don't immediately answer, "No." Some questions will be friendly—trying to help you out. Others will be concealed arguments directed at other judges. Even those that flag weaknesses in your position are not necessarily hostile. The judge may be troubled by the point and wants help in thinking it through.

Pause and think before answering. If you are uncomfortable with silence, you might blurt out something stupid. Instead:

"Good question. Let me think."

"Your Honor, I haven't considered that. Rather than try to come up with an answer on the spot, I would be happy to file a supplemental brief on it."

Finally never tell a judge to shut up.

"Your Honor, I will answer your question in a few minutes. Right now I would like to repeat what I said to the bathroom mirror."

"Dude, like I covered that in footnote twenty-three."

Be Candid

There is no need to win every skirmish. Conceding some points builds rapport and allows you to to focus on those that matter.

"Yes, my opponent is correct, the case did hold that. However, we believe that it is distinguishable."

"It is true, Your Honor, if you were to hold for my client certain expectations may be upset, but we believe that they may not be as extensive as feared because of the following limiting features."

Ethical rules require citation of adverse "controlling authority." Go further. Disclose the cases and statutes that you would like to consider if the decision were yours.

Use effective transitions

Law is complicated stuff. Say you are arguing three points: A, B, and C. What is the relationship between them? To prevail must you win on A *and* B *and* C or can you prevail if you win on either A *or* B *or* C. It is quite helpful to sort out these relationships

"That concludes my discussion of A. To prevail I must also establish B."

"That concludes my discussion of A. To prevail, however, it will be enough if I establish B."

Responding to Slippery Slopes

"Mom, if you send me to my room for spilling the milk you'll send me to my room for everything and you'll never see me again."

Many legal arguments focus not on the merits of the decision but on where it might lead. Judges aren't just thinking about your case; they are thinking about the next one as well. Slippery slope arguments are everywhere—not only in legal argument, but also in negotiation: "We can't do that because it would create a bad precedent." Knowing how to respond to slippery slope arguments is worth the price of this book. There are *three* responses to all slippery slope arguments. Write them out. They will be on the final. (Yeah, but if *they're* on the final, *everything* will be on the final.)

1. Slopes have bumps and decisions can be limited.

   "I will send you to your room only when you deliberately do something I have asked you not to." You will sometimes see such language in opinions which acts to pre-distinguish them.

2. Some slopes may be worth the ride.

   "Never see you again? Great! I'll miss your teenage years."

3. All slippery slope arguments are *reversible*.

   "If I don't send you to your room for this, I'll never send you to your room for anything."

What you want done

Tell the court what you want it *to do*. Remand the case, order a new trial? Do you want an order for some particular relief? Be prepared to answer: "Assuming we agree with your position on the law, what do you want us to do? Let's assume you've won. What should the last paragraph of our opinion say?"

Abandon your darlings

In writing you must murder some; in oral argument you might abandon some. Don't feel compelled to cover all the points you planned. An ideal oral argument is a *conversation* between you and the judges on a difficult legal matter. Like all good conversations, they cannot be charted in advance. New insights and new arguments will be triggered and the concerns of the judges might actually be answered. Committed to saying at least something about Point 3 you might cut off your opportunity to help the judges understand why you should win Point 2.

As to our Point 3. . . . Time!

Part A: Trial Preparation

TRIAL PREVIEW AND CHECKLIST

We have divided trial skills into two parts: preparation and execution.

Preparation:

> Lay Basic Plans; Prepare Your Witnesses: Practice Questions; Prepare for Problem Witnesses; Review Objections

Execution:

> Jury Selection; Opening Statement; Direct, Cross; Closing Argument

Stephen King, before editing a longer book, will polish off a couple of shorter ones—but he doesn't have a day job. Still, it is a great idea to finish your trial preparation early, knock off for a couple of days, and then go back and see what you have. You'll get a good sense of the forest, and you'll spot some troubling trees.

As a preview of what's to come, or as a last minute checklist, the following will give you a good idea of the points we will stress. If you are familiar with all of this, proceed to Advanced Placement and buy yourself a longer and sadder book.

The Plan

Do you have a plan? A theme? A legal theory? Do you know your strengths? Weaknesses? And what about lunch?

Basic Skills

Can you recognize *leading* questions? Can you ask *non-leading questions* that do not call for a narrative ("So, Dude, talk to me") by setting parameters ("After you got the tattoo, but before the nose ring, what did your parents say?") Are you familiar with the importance of silence in focusing attention? Are you familiar with the common trial objections? Are you aware when *not* to make them (particularly *leading* and *lack of foundation)*? Will you *listen* to the answers, always ready to go off in *new* directions?

Basic Choices

Will you draw the sting? What are the benefits and what are the costs?

Will you scatter bits of evidence to tie up in one grand finale or will you tie them up as you go?

As to the *order* of your witnesses and questions have you *considered* alternative approaches?

Are you sensitive to the dangerous risk of "opening the door"? (Opening the doors is the advocate's worst nightmare except the one about being eaten by a dinosaur.)

Have you read the disclosure? At least twice? Have you read the disclosure?

Telling a Good Story

Will the jury live the events as did your client? Will the jurors, who have no prior knowledge of the conflict, follow your case? Repetition is virtue, not vice.

Will your story be believed? Will you include *details*? Things witnesses *did*? Are there ways to make it more dramatic? Suspenseful? Would demonstrative evidence (charts, documents, re-enactments, toes) help?

Witness Prep

Have you discussed anxiety, and the prohibitions against hearsay and speculation?

Warned against being too partisan? Explained the importance of redirect? Cautioned against opening the door ("I know the defendant never committed any crimes") and causing a mistrial ("And not only that, the defendant has a lot of insurance")? Should your witnesses review prior testimony or writings? Do you want your experts to sit down or stand at the whiteboard with a pointer?

Jury Selection

Have you thought about the kind of jurors you want? Have you thought about the jurors you don't want? Will you involve your client in deciding on the preempts? Do you have voir dire questions that will flag things you don't want discussed in the jury room: "I don't believe in pain and suffering."

"Why not 'beyond a strong suspicion'?"

Do you know what's it like to be a goldfish?

Objection: Irrelevant!

We will tie it up.

Opening Statement

Is your goal to give a clear road map, or is it to focus on specific key issues? Will you avoid "argument"?

Should you have a theme? Should you repeat it often? Can your adversary turn it on you? How do you handle the issue of clarity versus suspense? Do you avoid promising too much?

Would charts or PowerPoint help?

Will you talk slow enough, use effective pauses but no big words? Will you look upon jurors as law professors in disguise, ready to leap, or as friends who have a difficult decision to make?

Direct Examination

Will you effectively personalize your witnesses? Will you get them comfortable talking, as opposed to grunting "yes," by asking non-leading questions as to preliminary matters?

Does the order of your questions make the most sense? You need not go chronologically, and your first and last questions are key.

Have you considered drama as well as clarity? Details and actions create belief. Do you lay adequate foundations (even if you can get away without them)? Would demonstrative evidence help?

As to *each* witness, what objections do you anticipate? How will you respond? Do any evidence problems jump out? If so, do you have a memo in support of your position, *citing* a controlling *case* or *statute*. Better still, *bring* the case or statute. Don't wing it; be prepared with the law. Judges take their jobs seriously.

Cross Examination

While the opposing witness is testifying on *direct*, your most common objections will be *hearsay*, *speculation*, *lack of foundation*, and *leading*. Can you recognize improper questions? Can you, right now, come up with a couple of examples of each?

As to your cross, do you avoid the sin of simply allowing the witness to repeat all of the damning testimony she gave on direct? ("Yes, I am sure of that! Really sure! Scouts' honor. Hope to die!")

Do you know the virtue of leading questions? Can you ask them nicely? Meanly?

Can the opposing witness *help* your case?

If you are attacking the *witness* (bias, perception, recall), is your theory mistake or perjury?

If you are attacking the *story*, will you (1) try to establish inconsistent details, (2) take it on directly by seeking bedrock, or (3) try to confuse the witness with slash and burn? What will you do if witnesses are evasive? Let them ramble, repeat the question, or curse your fate?

Are you familiar with the procedure to impeach with a prior inconsistent statement?

Closing argument

Are you prepared to throw off your rehearsed opening and begin with something you just thought of or by responding to something outrageous your opponent just said or did?

Is your overall structure the best? Why do you start, and finish, where you do?

Is your goal to marshal the evidence, or to focus on a few key issues? Is it to deny the validity of the evidence? Or is it to admit the evidence but give the jurors a new way to think about it ("The glass wasn't half full; it was just too small!")

Are you being too candid? Too contentious?

Do you supply arguments and stake out positions (sometimes in somewhat extreme form) so that your allies on the jury will have an easier time of it? Will you direct your arguments to all the jurors or just a few?

Are your metaphors fresh? Do your analogies work? Are your stock arguments flawed or stale?

IRS transitions Introduce the topic you are about to address, Relate it to the last topic you discussed, and indicate its Significance. Do you use them between your topics so that the jury will understand the relationship between them: is it an "and" or an "or"?

Are you clear on how each point fits? If you aren't being *explicit* in your argument, do you have a good reason not to be?

Can your argument be improved with visuals?

Do you run the risk of misstating evidence? Of putting yourself at issue? Is your argument overly emotional so as to draw an objection or alienate jurors?

And, perhaps most important of all, will you bore everyone to tears by going on and on, by *repeating* and *repeating* your arguments? Repetition is *not* always a virtue.

Do you have a great opening line?

"My client awoke to find himself turned into a giant cockroach."

Do you have a great closing line?

"My client never wanted to be a giant cockroach; he wanted to be a good dog."

PLANNING (BACKWARDS) AND STRATEGIC CHOICES

Start at the end and retreat to the beginning; start with the stars and retreat to the Big Bang, start with closing argument and retreat to "Call your first witness."

Einstein once said that genius is 1% inspiration, 99% perspiration; Wellington said that Waterloo was won on the playing fields of Eton. So what? They weren't lawyers. Trial advocacy courses are wonderful but send the wrong message—trials are won or lost in the preparation, not in the techniques.

Planning Backwards

Backwards planning is, ironically, straightforward. You figure out where you want to go and then work backwards to figure out a path to get there. Many lawyers we know begin each case by working on the summation. As new facts, law or other revelations emerge, that summation is guaranteed to morph—it's always a work in progress. But it remains the path to the beginning.

You need to do some background work. Read, reread, the pleadings, police and expert reports, and the disclosure. If the case involves a scene, *visit:* there is really no other way to get a physical sense of what happened and there will be no way to effectively cross-examine eye witnesses. Then there is the law. Start at the end. Review the form jury instructions. Then the statutes. Can you offer new jury instructions? Your ultimate goal will emerge, here to convince the jury to conclude:

The defendant was acting in self defense (as defined by the jury instructions).

What is the path? This conclusion rests upon key facts. Make a list:

The victim had a knife.

The victim had a reputation for violence.

The defendant knew of that reputation.

The victim shouted, "My grandmother most certainly does not wear cowboy boots."

These facts rest upon the *evidence you can prove*—testimony, exhibits, documents. Make another list—how to prove each fact.

Evidence supporting Victim had a knife.

Bartender's testimony

The knife ... Officer Jones

Witness Smith's testimony

Victim's girlfriend (on cross)

Evidence supporting Victim's reputation

Bartender

Witness Jones

Almost home. Time to make a list of witnesses and what you want to cover with each. Consider how to make their testimony more believable, (personalize and lay adequate foundations—how they know what they know), how to make the testimony more compelling (never underestimate the power of emotions), how your opponent will attack them on cross, whether you can meet the attack, and if there are any evidence problems.

Bartender

Saw victim's knife

Show how she was able to see knife

Visit Bar

Victim's reputation for violence

Common knowledge around bar

Check evidence code re reputation evidence

Possible cross of Bartender:

Her prior felony

Can I keep it out? Check Evidence Code re prior convictions.

Should I draw the sting? Opening statement or during direct?

What about your adversary's witnesses? Another list.

Victim's girlfriend

How can I use this witness to help *my case?*

Knows victim carried a knife

How can she harm?

Victim retreating and no knife in hand

How can I meet the harmful testimony?

Number of drinks

Much confusion

Loves victim

How can I keep certain testimony out?

Of course no one does it this way and neither will you. Trial preparation is a fluid, circular process. Reading the statute, a question for the girlfriend will pop into your mind; making a list of questions for the bartender will loop you back to the jury instructions and trigger another question for the girlfriend. And the preparation doesn't end with "Call your first witness" but rather with "We rest."

"After every witness, things change. Every night I reread the disclosure, witness statements, police reports. I must read them all seven or eight times during a trial. Every time I find something new and important."

Now you have the raw data. You must shape it into a compelling story and you will face difficult choices at every turn. Here are three: Should you take the sting out? Should you be a bull in the China shop? And in what order will you present your case?

What order?

Well, who is your first witness? What is your last question? Most importantly, *why* did you make those choices?

Traditional advice is to put your two strongest witnesses first and last and end on a high note. We remember most what we hear first and last. Chronological stories are easy but dull. You are telling a story. Make it interesting. Sure, the stay in the hospital was the last event but isn't the terrifying crash more compelling?

You face choices in attacking your opponent's case as well. In the case of the girlfriend, during your cross, should you develop the favorable material (she knew the victim carried a knife) before you attack the harmful testimony? Whatever you decide, have a reason;

it doesn't even have to be good reason, just something you carefully considered.

Sleuth or Bull?

There is a lot to be said for presenting many somewhat disjointed facts and then, at the very end, bringing them all together in a forceful and memorable flash.

1. If it is unclear where you are going, your opponent will have a hard time responding.

2. If the jurors on their own come to the conclusion you want them to ("The butler did it") then Hog Heaven. They will defend it with passion.

3. You avoid the nay-sayer problem. If you begin with your conclusion ("The butler did it") and then offer your supporting clues, some jurors will be inclined to sit back and think, "Nope, that doesn't fit."

On the other hand confusion can be a major problem: if jurors don't see the relevance of the evidence when it is presented, it might be ignored. Jurors often decide long before closing arguments; it is always easier to convince people as an initial matter than it is to get them to change their minds.

The call is yours. In your opening statement, how much of your case will you present? On direct, will you tie up the witness' testimony to the theory of your case or scatter bits? During closing, will you be explicit as to the conclusions you want the jurors to come to or will you be implicit, hoping that the jurors figure things out themselves?

Drawing the sting

"You testified that the defendant was with you the night in question. Are you his mother?"

Drawing the sting suggests that the information really isn't that harmful, you brought it up after all. This makes a lot of sense. But don't go overboard. It does *not* prevent your adversary from rejoicing:

"So, you're his <u>mother</u>? And you love him and want to help him, isn't that right?"

It also gives your opponent an open shot. Jurors resent lawyers beating up witnesses (particularly mothers) and hence there is a cost in suggesting the witness is so biased as to lie. By bringing up the matter yourself, your adversary need not bear this cost.

Finally it some cases your adversary may not even realize there is a string to use or decide not to use it.

Related to this issue is the matter of *filling holes*. If there is a fatal flaw in your case, clear it up. Take Hansel and Gretel: if the house was made of candy, why no ants?

If you don't explain this, expect from your adversary on closing:

"Ladies and Gentlemen of the Jury, where were the ants?"

Still worse a juror, during deliberation:

"You know folks, one thing that bothers me about the story, no ants."

Your goose is cooked! (Sorry.)

Creating a Trial Notebook

Once you have decided all that you need to decide, create a trial notebook. A trial notebook is simply a way to keep things organized. Consider creating a chart for each witness that lays out the topics you want to cover, what evidence you want to introduce or keep out, the legal arguments and references you anticipate, the clever asides you want to make. Have a section that organizes your exhibits so that you can access them quickly without any annoying shuffling of paper. "*Your Honor, can I have a moment to find Exhibit 42 in this disorganized mess in front of me?*" is not cool. Picking up Exhibit 42 in an nano-second and smoothly confronting the witness about her prior inconsistent statement is cool.

PREPARE YOUR WITNESSES

Q. And lastly, Gary, all your responses must be oral. O.K.? What school do you go to?

A. Oral.

Q. How old are you?

A. Oral.

Preparing witnesses is an act of fine tuning. Too much preparation and your witnesses appear scripted. Too little and your witnesses an appear as lost as Gary.

You don't want Cheerleaders

When two ships collide almost invariably all the crew on one ship will testify in unison against the opposing crew, and, what is more significant, such passengers as happen to be on either ship will almost invariably be found corroborating the stories of their respective crews.

So wrote Francis Wellman in his 1920s classic, *The Art of Cross Examination*. Sea travel has improved but humanity hasn't. Witnesses attempt to explain away damaging admissions and gladly volunteer hurtful tidbits *without* being asked ("Yes, I saw the defendant leave his car. Then he went over an kicked a puppy.") No one ever believes cheerful cheerleaders.

"Don't worry. My case rests on more than your testimony. If on cross you have to admit something that hurts us, don't try to explain it away. Explanations just get you in trouble and make you look like someone who is trying to influence the jury. Remember that I have redirect and I can ask for the explanation then. An just answer my questions; don't try to stick in knives. If it's important, I'll ask about the puppy."

Don't meet with your witnesses together

Q (on cross): Now isn't it true that you met with the other witnesses to discuss what you were going to testify?

Witnesses, consciously or unconsciously, will try to make their testimony consistent with that of others: that's when they get into trouble on cross. Even if they don't trip, if all the witnesses tell the identical story it comes off as rehearsed, or worse.

Tell your witnesses it is okay for them to have talked with you concerning their testimony. Tell them to tell the truth. If the other lawyer asks what they were told, "I was told to tell the truth."

Where to look and how to testify

> *"The jury will be trying to figure out if you really know what you are saying and if they can trust you. It is better for you to answer my questions in sentences, not just in grunts and nods. Talk to the jury; if you talk to a juror in the back, you will talk loud enough. On cross, if you get a difficult question, don't look at me, it smacks of cheating. Talk slowly."*

On cross, things are pretty much reversed. Narration is generally a bad idea; the more that is said, the more to attack. While short answers are preferred, it is perfectly proper for a witness to explain an answer if a simple *yes* or *no* would be misleading.

> *"Before you answer a question, pause to make sure you understand it, answer only the question and don't volunteer information. Don't look at the opposing lawyer who can be intimidating. Look at the jury or the back of the courtroom. You will want to convince the lawyer that you are right; forget it."*

Discuss hearsay, speculation and inadmissible evidence

When witnesses testify without getting into objectionable material, things will go smoother and likely the judge will allow them more room to narrate. Lay witnesses can only testify to what they saw, heard, felt, tasted or smelled. They cannot base their testimony on what others have told them nor can they base it on speculation. Explain this to your witnesses. If they know something that is inadmissible, caution them not to blurt it out.

Discuss depositions, documents, and demonstrations

If you are going to have the witness physically demonstrate something, or write on the board, *rehearse!* Otherwise disaster.

Should your witnesses read their prior testimony and be familiar with any documents that might come into play? Probably as that will refresh their memories and avoid a lot of silly inconsistencies. On the other hand what you *show* your client and your witnesses to refresh their recollections *may be subject to disclosure.* Check your local rules.

Objections

"Sometimes I will object only to slow things down if I think you are getting in trouble. Think and slow down." Some believe that such an objection is improper as there is no substantive justification for it. Others don't. (How's that for taking a stand?)

Rehearsals

Roleplay at least some questions, if simply to allow the witness to get a feel for the format and to allow you to get a sense of how the witness answers questions. Does the witness speak too quickly? Too softly? A *roleplay of cross might help.* Having another lawyer do it is probably best; it adds realism and allows you to observe what happens. Does the witness *listen carefully* to the question? *Pause* before answering? Answer *only* the question and not volunteer?

Rehearse, but not too much. If you are unsure of what the witness might say, as in the case of most criminal defendants, go over all of the testimony. Otherwise, probably not a good idea. Surely you can tell witnesses the areas you will explore and get a general sense of how they will respond. However, you will want a lively presentation: people are much more spontaneous, and believable, when they are in the moment, answering questions rather than trying to remember their previous answers.

Actors improve with rehearsals; the rest of us are not Prince Hamlet nor were meant to be.

PRACTICE YOUR QUESTIONS

Good questions are our musical scales, our jump shots, things to practice and practice so that they become routine, so that they are there when we need them.

Be Interested and Listen. On *direct* you *know* the answer and might appear bored. Recapture the excitement—the fear—of the first time you asked the question, when a bad answer would destroy your case, and a good answer would send you around the room in a victory lap.

Asking questions on *cross,* the danger is failing to *listen.*

> *Q: It is a fact, is it not, that you ran the stop sign?*
>
> *A: Well, yes, I did overshoot the stop sign a little. You see, my brakes have been out for some time.*
>
> *Q:* (reading from his yellow pad) *Now, in fact, your car stopped about ten feet into the intersection, isn't that right?*

Be prepared to go off in new directions. Digest the answer before moving on. Count to three.

One Question, One Fact. Because we know what happened, we might summarize:

> *Q: So you were badly mistreated by your stepsisters, but somehow got to the Ball anyway where you had a pretty good time and hung out with a charming prince and then you lost one of your shoes?*

As a *technical* matter, it is objectionable for many reasons. It is a *compound* question as it contains more than one fact. It is also a *leading* question and, most probably, *assumes facts not in evidence* unless the various predicates were already established (not all princes are charming). But the main problem with the question isn't technical.

The basic flaws with the question are that it condenses a great story into a blur and you are telling the story instead of the witness. It takes time to process information; the jurors will be with the bad relatives while you're dancing at the ball. And the jurors will be assessing your credibility when you want your well-prepared witness to shine.

> *Q: How were you treated by your step sisters?*
>
> *Q: Did you get to the Ball?*
>
> *Q: What kind of time did you have?*
>
> *Q: Did you meet anyone special?*
>
> *Q: After the dance, did anything strange happen?*
>
> *Q: Do you have a promotional contract with any shoe company?*

Types of Questions

There are different kinds of questions: *open* and *closed*, *leading* and *non-leading*. *Open* questions *cannot* be answered "yes" or "no." They force witnesses to talk.

> *Q: Where would you rather be?*

Closed questions *can*, but need not, be answered "yes" or "no."

> *Q: Would you rather be in Philadelphia?*

Leading questions *suggest* how the witness should answer.

> *Q: You'd rather be in Philadelphia, wouldn't you?*
>
> *Q: Does W.C. Field's tombstone read, "I'd rather be in Philadelphia?"*

Although the last question does not *explicitly* suggest how the witness should answer the question, it is nonetheless *leading* as it supplies the witness with important details that may be at issue.

On direct, non-leading questions

There are a few times leading questions are permissible during direct: going over preliminary and non-contested matters, sometimes questioning children and when a good witness goes bad, either by forgetting or turning hostile. Now let's look at the case for asking non-leading questions (even when leading ones might be permitted).

> *Q: You love your kids, correct?*
>
> *A: Yes.*

Q: In fact, they are the most important things in your life.

A: Yes.

Q: And you would never inflict unnecessary pain on them.

A: No.

These are all leading questions as they either suggest how the witness is to answer or remind the witness of things to say. Worse than objectionable, they are stupid. The lawyer is testifying, not the witness. The lawyer is denying the witness the opportunity to tell his story to the jury, in his own words, with his own emotions. The jurors will not get a sense of him and will have a harder time in assessing his credibility.

On direct, ask *open* questions, questions which cannot be answered with a simple "yes" or "no", questions which *force* your witnesses to give the key testimony in a way that lets the jury evaluate their candor and recall. However, there is the problem of jumping into the fire. Fearful of asking leading questions, you might ask questions which are so vague as to be objectionable as either *vague* or *calling for a narrative.*

Say you want to establish that on November 17th the defendant told the witness that he was going to commit treason. You can't ask:

Q: On November 17th, did the defendant tell you that he was going to commit treason?

That would be a leading question. Even though it does not suggest an answer ("Didn't he?"), it reminds the witness of key details. So, to avoid the leading problem, you might ask:

Q: What happened on November 17th of last year?

This is a non-leading, open-ended question. It suggests no answer and forces the witness to answer in his own words. It *seems* perfectly permissible. However, some open-ended questions are objectionable because they offer no guidance to the witness as to the parameters of the answer.

The problem with narratives is that the opposing lawyer will not know what roads the witness might take, roads that might involve *hearsay*, *speculation* or matters previously determined to be *inadmissible.* By objecting to this question, the proponent would then have to take the witness through the key events of the incident so that specific objections could be made, such as hearsay, lack of foundation, or improper opinion.

Another problem with narrative answers is that they may come across as memorized. Good idea is to occasionally break the narrative.

To avoid the vagueness objection, set parameters on the question:

> Q: *After the accident, before the police arrived, what happened?*
>
> Q: *After the tattoo, but before you got the nose ring, what did your parents say?*

On Cross, leading questions

Leading questions *aren't questions*, are they? *They are statements of fact followed by a question mark.* Reread the last sentence: it is the root of the whole enterprise.

Leading questions are marvelous. Not only do they help you control the evasive witness, they also allow you to tell *your* story with no distracting clutter offered by the witness. In a negligence case, assume that an adverse witness has testified that your client, the defendant, ran a red light. On cross, you wish to develop some favorable testimony: the road was wet, and the defendant applied the brakes before entering the intersection. On cross, there is simply no need, as there is on direct, to lay a foundation for the testimony by putting the witness on the scene and so forth. You simply go for it:

> Q: *The road was wet, wasn't it?*
>
> Q. *Isn't it true that the defendant applied his brakes before he entered the intersection?*

Cross *doesn't* mean angry. Leading questions are *not necessarily hostile.* Reread that last sentence; it is the root of the enterprise. Leading questions can be friendly. Basically you are making a statement and merely asking the witness to confirm or deny it. You can do so in an accusatory tone of voice, implying that the factual statement is harmful to the witness, or in a friendly tone of voice, suggesting that the fact helps the witness.

Whatever your tone (accepting or rejecting), *your voice should not go up at the end.* Reread the last sentence. When we ask questions, our voices go up at the end, thus inviting a response. In declaratory sentences, our voice drops at the end, thus inviting nothing. On cross, you are not inviting responses, you are making statements. Learn to ask leading questions, not as questions, but as statements: keep your voice flat at the end.

Scales to Practice, Grounders to Field

Recall Cinderella, the short version.

> *Q: So you were badly mistreated by your stepsisters, but somehow got to the Ball anyway where you had a pretty good time and hung out with the charming prince, and then you lost one of your shoes?*

Although some judges may disagree, trials are not time trials. You don't have to leap over tall buildings in a single bound. *Take baby steps* to get there—one fact at a time. It is so much easier for a jury to follow and it builds the drama.

1. Break the Cinderella question into a series of one-fact questions. How many can you get?

2. Assume you are conducting Cinderella's *direct*. Write out a series of questions that would cover the main points but would be neither leading nor too vague. Try asking the questions in a tone that suggests you *don't know* the answers and that your life hangs in the balance. Keep your questions small—one piece of the story at a time.

3. Assume you are conducting a *cross* of Cinderella. You have come up with the following leading questions.

> *Q: Your step sisters had been treating you badly, isn't that true?*
>
> *Q: Despite this, you got to the Ball, correct?*
>
> *Q: And you can't deny you were having a pretty good time, can you?*
>
> *Q: You met a young prince, right?*
>
> *Q: And you found him charming?*
>
> *Q: You lost a shoe, isn't that a fact?*

Practice asking these questions, making sure that your voice does not go up at the end. You are really making statements, not asking questions. The first time through, ask the questions with a tone of voice that suggests these facts in no way reflect badly on Cinderella. Then go through them again with a tone of voice that suggests that Cinderella is a self-promoting brat.

> *Q: And you have sold your story to Nike, isn't that so, well, 21st century?*

Use Ordinary Language

> *Q. Mrs. Jones, is your appearance this morning pursuant to a deposition notice which I sent to your attorney?*
>
> *A. No. This is how I dress when I go to work.*

Speak in plain English. Don't confuse the jury and don't embarrass your witness.

> Lawyer: *What transpired next?*
>
> Witness: *What?*
>
> Lawyer: *What transpired next?*
>
> Witness: *Sorry, I don't understand.*
>
> Judge: *What happened next?*

PROBLEM WITNESSES

Your witnesses may freeze up, and opposition witnesses can be evasive or change their testimony. What to do about them apples?

Forgetful, nervous, and run-on

Despite your efforts at preparing them, some of your witnesses simply go berserk. If so, *break out of role*, stop asking questions, and *talk* to the witness.

> *Nervous witness*: "Now everyone gets nervous testifying for the first time. We all understand. Just take your time."
>
> *Unclear witness*: "I think the jury is having a hard time following. Slow down."
>
> *Run-on witness (cutting off)*: "That's enough. I believe you answered my question." (Or, "Who asked you to testify?")

If a witness forgets, *ask a few leading questions* to get her back on track. But lead only as to collateral and non-contested matters. You never want to lead a witness over key testimony. You want the witness to testify and the solution is to *refresh recollection*.

You can refresh recollection by showing the witness just about anything: a newspaper article, a deposition, a bowl full of mush. The document is *hearsay* and, unless otherwise admissible (as a business record, for example), it is not admissible. It should *not* be read into evidence. The only reason the witness can *silently* read it is to help refresh *current* recollection.

> *"Having read the newspaper story, do you* ***now*** *recall what happened on that day?"*

At this point your opponent can take the witness on *voir dire* to test whether the witness actually recalls what happened or is simply recounting what she read. If the latter, it is inadmissible hearsay.

Evasive Witnesses

Like law students taking exams, witnesses on cross like to answer *their* questions, not yours. The essential thing is to *look* at the witness and *listen* to the response. Don't be looking at your note pad, rehearsing your next question. Has the witness answered your question?

Q: Dish, you ran away with the spoon, didn't you?

A: The times were out of joint. The cow had just jumped over the moon.

Repeating the question usually works, *"That's not what I asked. Let me try again, Dish you ran away from the spoon, didn't you?"* A simple, *"Please answer my questions"* will also usually do the trick. But, before that, realize that it might be a good idea to let the witness continue to evade your questions. Evasive witnesses lose credibility. Why is it Dish wants to *duck* the question. (Sorry.) Is there something to hide?

Evasive witnesses are often making things up on the fly and really don't know where they are going. Consider pursuit.

Q: What do you mean, time was out of joint?

Q: "So, just where did the cow land?"

Or you can appeal to higher authority:

"Your Honor, instruct the witness to answer 'yes' or 'no.' "

Most judges won't and will allow witnesses considerable leeway in explaining their answers. A series of short questions can work wonders:

Q: I didn't ask you about the times. Did I?

Q: I didn't ask you about the cow. Did I?

Q: Do you remember what I asked you?

Don't underestimate the power of repeating a question, slightly changed.

Q. Did you ever stay all night with this man in New York?

A. I refuse to answer that question.

Q. Did you ever stay all night with this man in Chicago?

A. I refuse to answer that question.

Q. Did you ever stay all night with this man in Miami?

A. No

In our discussion of cross-examination we will discuss how you might prevent evasions by bluff and by closing doors.

Impeaching with prior statements

The darling of trial advocacy courses is overrated. Jurors realize, as we did before law school, that people describe events differently on different occasions and that memories are never constant. In fact, inconsistency can be argued as a test of truth:

> *Ladies and Gentlemen of the Jury, we know that the witness was telling the truth because he told it as he remembered it, even though he knew that he had made somewhat inconsistent statements before. If he was lying, he would have told you exactly what he said during his deposition.*

Impeach with inconsistencies *only* if it will help; don't do it simply because you know how. The inconsistencies should be sharp and material.

If the witness *denies* the prior statement, then, as long as it is material, you can prove it up. If the judge rules the matter to be collateral, you *cannot* prove it up. If the witness *admits* the prior inconsistent statement, then that's pretty much it. Move on.

We will not bore you (or ourselves) with the mechanics of this. Consult Tom Mauet, *Fundamentals of Trial Advocacy* (a longer and less happy book). One thing he recommends is that, before getting to the prior inconsistency, you recommit the witness to the current version.

> *Q: On direct you testified that the Little Old Lady whispered "hush."*
>
> *A: Yes, she did.*
>
> *Q: Whispered, "hush."*
>
> *A: Yes.*

Some might disagree with this. The witness might be able to wiggle out.

> *Q: On direct you testified that the Little Old Lady whispered "hush."*
>
> *A: What I meant to say is that she's a lush.*

OBJECTIONS

Common Objections

Lack of Foundation

Before a witness can testify to what she saw, heard, touched, tasted or smelled, it must be shown that she was in a position to see, hear, touch, taste or smell. To testify that the defendant ran the red light: she was at the scene, saw the car enter the intersection and saw the color of the light. Foundation for *expert opinion*, qualification and the need for expert opinion. As to a *document*, its authentication. For criminal confessions, *Miranda* and voluntariness. *Lack of foundation* sniffs out testimony that may rest on improper foundations: hearsay (what another witness told her) and speculation (given the position of the cars, the defendant must have run the light).

Hearsay

"I heard," "I read," "Everyone knows," "He said," and even "*I* said" should put you on alert. Hearsay is a statement (a) made out of court and (b) offered for the truth. Offered for something else isn't hearsay. When your adversary's witnesses are testifying, ask yourself: "How do they *know*?" I am sure your remember all of the exceptions to that rule, such as the Dying Lawyer Declaration. *Useful exceptions abound*—business records, prior testimony, excited utterance. Some require that the witness be unavailable—statement against interest, former testimony. And party admissions aren't hearsay at all.

Speculation

From a lay witness, anything that begins "I think," "I feel," or "It seems to me" is suspect. "He feels" or "she thought" is off the charts.

Improper Opinion

Lay witnesses *cannot* offer their opinions *except* when they can: if their opinion is "*rationally based on the perception of the witness and is helpful to a clear understanding of the witness' testimony or the determination of a fact in issue.*" *(Federal Rules of Evidence 70).* For example a witness can testify "He was drunk." This opinion can be bolstered by having the witness testify also to what he saw (staggering), heard (blood oaths) and, unfortunately, how he smelled. Expert opinion must "*assist the trier of fact to understand the evidence or to determine a fact in issue.*" If the jurors can figure things out themselves, expert testimony is objectionable.

Irrelevant

Does the testimony make more or less probable a fact at issue? Admitting irrelevant evidence is no great sin, it just takes time and perhaps creates confusion. But wary of "she did it before, so it must be true now." That's irrelevant but powerfully persuasive.

Unduly Prejudicial

This is the objection when the evidence is *too* relevant (gruesome pictures, severed toes) whose *probative value is substantially outweighed by the danger of unfair prejudice, confusion of issues, or misleading the jury. (Federal Rule 403)*

Argumentative

Q: You expect the jury to believe that?

Q: Are you lying now or were you lying then?

Q: Does your grandmother still wear cowboy boots?

Asked and answered

You can't ask the same question again and again to stress the answer. Of course, on cross you can ask questions already answered on direct, and on direct you can repeat some questions in order to go back and pick up a line of inquiry.

Leading

Does the question suggest to the witness how he should answer? This can occur by either a statement followed by, "isn't that right?" or a question which supplies key facts with no explicit suggestion as to how to answer. You can lead on cross but not on direct.

Calls for a Narrative/ Vague questions

A question should be specific enough to tell the witness—and your opponent—the general contours of what you want. Your opponent should know enough about what's coming so that she can interpose an objection before it gets out.

Non responsive

This objection can be made only by the person asking the question.

Compound

Questions which put in play more than one fact.

"Wasn't this chapter short, happy, and helpful?"

Remember: *one fact, one question.*

Should you object?

Never object just because you can. Losing objections *almost* always hurts. Object too often, the jury will find you an annoying little chatterbox. Object and are overruled, you have put the evidence in **bold**. Object and are sustained, often your opponent will simply rephrase the question and the evidence comes in stronger, clearer, and more believable.

Object if you have a good shot at keeping the evidence out: *Hearsay, improper opinion, speculation, unduly prejudicial,* are the clear cases. Even if you don't keep the evidence out you have protected the record. Pause before objecting on other grounds.

The more the lawyer *leads*, the less the witness testifies and this harms credibility. Further, a sustained objection simply requires the lawyer to ask a few non-leading questions to get to the same spot. On the other hand, if you think the witness will not be able to answer the question without being lead, object.

As to *lack of foundation,* object only if you think there isn't a good one and thus you can keep the evidence out. However, if you know the witness's testimony rests on a good one, but the lawyer forgot to lay it, don't object. If you do, what once was shaky now becomes a pyramid.

As to *vague* and *compound* questions, they may be doing the questioner more harm than good. A focused, damning response to a vague question suggests partisanship and compound questions confuse the witness and the jury.

To protect your witness on cross, you might want to object to slow things down and give your witness time to think.

"Your Honor, I fail to see the relevance of this line of questioning."

"Your Honor, would counsel allow the witness to answer the question?"

"Irrelevant" is often used as a ploy to alert a witness on cross that those innocent questions being asked aren't quite so innocent. The response: "Your Honor, I will tie up in a few more questions." However it is bush to object time and time again just to throw a beginner off their game. Juries (hopefully) will resent this.

In short, don't object because it is there; *only object if you have a good reason*. On the other hand, *don't fail to object* because you can't think of a category.

"Your Honor, I object, counsel is being overly dramatic."

We are not dealing with precise legal categories. The Federal Rules do not mention such objections as "compound question," "asked and answered," "non-responsive," "argumentative." Rather, Rule 611 simply instructs the judge

> *to exercise reasonable control over the mode and order of interrogating witnesses and presenting evidence so as to (1) make the interrogation and presentation effective for the ascertainment of the truth, (2) avoid needless consumption of time, and (3) protect witnesses from harassment or undue embarrassment.*

Traditional objections are justified under this broad language, and they are not exhaustive. An overly dramatic attorney may be getting in the way of the "ascertainment of the truth."

Have a list of common objections at counsel table. Stand when you make an objection. The witness might actually shut up.

Object when it will do you the most good. If you can object before trial, file a *motion in limine*. That will give the judge time to research and agree with you and not make a bad call on the spur of the moment. And you'll know before trial what's what.

Object before the witness answers. "*The jury will disregard that statement*" makes it impossible to disregard. Right now, do not imagine an elephant. We dare you.

Responding to Objections

Don't assume your opponent is correct and go on to the next question. To preserve your right to appeal, you must first get the judge to rule. This may not be as easy. Your opponent objects, the judge nods. Nothing goes on the record. "Your Honor, are you sustaining my opponent's objection?" Experienced trial judges will nod vigorously.

Once you have the ruling on the record, generally it is also required that you make an *offer of proof* as to the substance of the excluded testimony.

Opponent: I object.

Court: Sustained.

You: Your Honor, I would like to make an offer of proof.

Court: Counsel for both sides, approach the bench.

You: (Softly so the jury won't hear) *Your Honor, this witness will testify . . . .*

Don't be stampeded when your opponent objects. On the other hand, don't automatically assume that your opponent is wrong and begin to argue. If you are to argue, remember, that the argument is *to* the judge, not *between* counsel; talk to the judge, not to your opponent.

When you get a bad call, move on

How many pitchers have had a melt-down because the umpire missed strike three? Don't brood. Think about the next pitch. Slider away.

How can we make this chapter happy? How about a dog story involving hearsay.

The witness saw a man crawling out a window and then a dog chasing him. The witness followed but lost contact momentarily but then came upon the dog at the base of the tree, barking at the defendant.

Lawyer: Objection your Honor. Hearsay. In effect the dog is testifying that the man in the tree is the same man crawling out the window.

Judge: But dogs don't lie.

Lawyer: Yes, your Honor. But they have a good sense of humor!

Part B: Game Day

JURY SELECTION, PRETRIAL MOTIONS AND WHERE TO SIT

Where to Sit

If you haven't had a trial before the assigned judge, spend a morning watching one. Best to watch a jury selection (does the judge question or do the lawyers?) and opening statements and one or two witnesses (must the lawyers stand behind the podium?). Introduce yourself to court personnel (and don't be pushy or pompous). They can correct your blunders (if they are so inclined) and are happy to answer your questions (everyone loves to give advice, we, apparently, more than most).

It is fine to introduce yourself to the judge but don't talk about the case you are to try. It is impermissible to *ex parte* a judge—talk about a case without your adversary being present.

Pretrial Motions

These can be used to for a variety of reasons, mostly to get advance rulings on disputed evidentiary matters. Judges are busy people. Long boilerplate motions often go unread. Be concise. Judges know the law. There is no need to recite the history of the Fourth Amendment. Get to the point.

Think of a pretrial motion as a way to get the judge in your camp. If your adversary hasn't made all the disclosures or made ridiculous offers, a good writer can get those in. Remember what we said about oral argument:

> *The statement of facts is not merely part of the argument, it is more often than not the argument itself.*

Jury Selection

> *Client: "Your Honor, I want a new lawyer. This one never pays any attention to me."*
>
> *Judge: "Counselor?"*
>
> *Lawyer: "Sorry your Honor, I wasn't paying any attention."*

Involve your clients in jury selection; their guess is as good as yours. The jurors are watching your interactions with your client and you don't want to be spotted moving away. Watch how the jurors react to you and your client. Scowls and glares are a clue.

Use jury selection as a opportunity. Even if you can't or don't get the jurors you want, you can accomplish a lot in jury selection. Use your questions to connect on a personal level with each juror. Use their names. Ask each of them something other than yes or no. [don't leave anybody out—when you spoke to 11 and the 12th is scowling at you, that's a hint.] Jury selection can be a conversation that creates a relationship between you and the jurors.

Preview your case with the jury. If it's an identification case, ask a juror: "*Have you ever seen anyone that you thought you knew but it turn out to be somebody else? Yes? Tell us about it.*"

What about the category approach?

"Personal injury plaintiffs want emotional, sympathetic types: Catholics, Southern Europeans, Irish, people who work with their hands. Civil defendants want hardheaded people: Germans, Norwegians, Presbyterians, bankers. Prosecutors want the same. Criminal defendants want people who have been oppressed: Blacks, Jews."

Our rule of thumb: As a prosecutor, try for 12 infuriated Prussians; for the defense, 12 drunken buffoons. With drunken Prussians and infuriated buffoons you're on your own.

Besides bigoted, the category approach rests on two questionable assumptions: that the jury make-up is critical, and, assuming it is, that we can predict human behavior.

How important is jury make-up? Would different juries would come to different verdicts? Jury deliberations burn a hot fire. Jurors take their jobs seriously. In law school we all laughed when we read of a judge instructing jurors to "disregard the previous answer." We laughed because we had never been on a jury.

Juror One: You remember what the cop said.

Juror Two: Yes, but the judge said we shouldn't consider that. Do you have any other reasons for your position?

Most judges are drum majors for juries. You will be if you read *Jury: The People v. Juan Corona* by Victor Villasenor. It recounts the 13 days the jury deliberated a murder. What strikes one is how seriously the jurors took their job: they had actually voted to convict on Day Twelve but decided to spend the night thinking if they had overlooked anything. What is also striking is how the jurors viewed the lawyers. They talked about the lawyers; they applauded their art, their ploys, their feints, and their rhetoric. But soon someone said, "Enough! Sure, they started a scene or two, were full of high sentence, a bit obtuse, but now let's look at the evidence."

Even if you are convinced that who gets on the jury can shift outcomes, how good are we at predicting human behavior?

Two Chinese philosophers paused beside a quiet pond in the Summer Palace.

"Look, the goldfish are swimming happily."

"You cannot know if they are happy. You are not a goldfish."

"You cannot know what I know. You are not me."

Good luck at knowing what the Devil Himself can't know, a person's heart. One thing you can do is anticipate things *you don't want discussed* in the jury room:

Juror: Look, the defendant is a big corporation and the plaintiff needs the money.

Juror: Yes, that's what the defendant says. But that nice young policeman was there and he says different, and I always believe what policemen say.

Juror: I just don't think people should be compensated for pain and suffering.

Juror: It's enough for me to convict because he had a drink before getting in the car.

Draft questions to flag these problems:

"The law allows awards for pain and suffering. Do you have any objection to that?"

Related to this is the problem of the *one person jury*. Say your case involves a dispute about the authenticity of an email. Experts on both sides will testify. You don't want an IT person on the jury who will render his or her opinion on the matter. Recall your first week in law school. Who did you believe? At Orientation the Dean, and assorted dancing bears (professors), told you what to expect. You didn't believe a word. Then they paraded out some practitioners. You began to listen. Finally, the student representatives. "Well," you said, "maybe there's some truth in what they say." The only person you *really* believed was another first year who you met in the bathroom who told you about a cousin whose good friend went to law school. With apologies to many of our readers, we call it "the guy at the next urinal" phenomenon.

Do you want jurors who are "like" your client? They would empathize and see the evidence somewhat differently than would jurors of dissimilar backgrounds. Sometimes, however, women are harder on, and less sympathetic, to women, and the same can be said of minorities judging minorities. Knowing that other jurors might suspect them of bias, they may lean over backwards.

Constitutional issues lurk in jury selection. It has been held that a black defendant was denied equal protection when the prosecutor used peremptory challenges to remove all blacks from the jury. Other cases have ruled gender discrimination impermissible.

Do the best you can. Ask yourself what kind of a juror you want on your case: Young? Smart? People who fall asleep? ("Ladies and Gentlemen, you didn't hear the prosecution offer one word of testimony concerning motive.") The best advice probably is to rely upon your *and* your client's gut reactions. Do you like the juror? Do you feel that the juror will listen to your side?

Post Game. If the judge allows it, talk to the jurors after their verdict. You will get a sense of how they viewed your witnesses and your arguments and you may find that the juror you dreaded most was your strongest ally.

Although this was billed as a happy book we must confess that one of the authors (we ain't telling), after his first trial talked with the jurors, letting it drop that it was indeed his first trial. Expecting high praise, instead, "Yeah, that's what we thought."

OPENING STATEMENT

Put yourself in the jury box. You have very little idea about what trials are like, except what you're seen on *CSI,* and virtually nothing about the case you are about to hear. You realize that, down the road you will have to make a very important decision, one that will change the lives of the people over there, sitting four or five feet from you. What would you like from the lawyers?

The leading appellate lawyer of his generation, John W. Davis, said the most important thing for a lawyer to have was a "*sincere and single desire to be helpful to the Court.*" How can you be helpful to the jury?

Road Maps and Storytelling

Opening statements are called "road maps." Tell the jury where you are going, what evidence you will produce, and how it all fits. Your first job, like other famous first jobs, is to create *order* out of *chaos.* Without a road map, the jury will get lost on an overpass near Albuquerque.

Trials are *not* about the witnesses, exhibits, or jury instructions. Trials are about *real people* and *real events*; the stuff of drama: explosions, murders, betrayal, and, in the case of commercial litigation, bad widgets.

Tell the story your client lived. Things that *are* happening are always more engrossing than things that *did* happen. If possible, use present tense. (As Groucho said, "We're past tense; we live in bungalows now.")

> *This case is about a life ruined by a drunk driver. Mary Worth is on her way home from work. She approaches the intersection of Elm and Main. The light is green. Suddenly, off to her left, headlights. They're coming fast. Will she be hit? Will she be killed?*

Good storytelling does *not* consist of flowery phrases, emotional outbursts, and vile maledictions. Good storytelling is simple and straightforward and uses nouns and verbs much more than adjectives and adverbs. Instead of lamenting the "great pain" your client has suffered, talk of the *specifics*: how often she must take painkillers, how often she must leave movies early, how often she wakes at night.

Themes

If in a couple of weeks a juror is asked, "What was the case about?" what answer would you want? That's your theme.

"It was about a life ruined by a drunk driver."

"Good themes are simple, universal, and timeless," writes Professor Tom Mauet. "They catch the ear, make a vivid and visceral connection, and send a clear message. They complete the sentences: 'This case is about __'; 'This happened because __'; 'We win because __.' " He points to simple but powerful words—love, hate, revenge, jealousy—and powerful short phrases: "keeping one's promise," "profit over people," "a good dog gone bad." Some advise that you state your theme at the top of your opening, refer to it a couple of times during your opening, and then work it into you ending.

In thinking about theme and how much to stress it, however, be aware of the brooding omnipresence of your adversary, ready to pounce and turn the tables. Novelists don't have that problem: "No Charles, it wasn't the best of times nor the worst of times; in fact the times were actually pretty mediocre."

Connecting with the Jury

Trials are not just about the plaintiffs, defendants and witnesses. They are also about you, the lawyer. You are the story teller. You are the one who conveys your client's message to the jurors. We all listen more closely to story tellers with whom we can relate. Use the opening statement to connect to the jury on a personal level. Be honest, direct and, above all, yourself. If you connect, your message is more likely to be heard and accepted.

Caveats on Storytelling

Be candid and consider suspense.

If the jury first hears from your opponent that Mary had been going 80 miles per hour, its favorable impression of your case, and, indeed, of you, will crash. This is another illustration of the "drawing the sting" dilemma. Do so if the failure to do so will lead the jurors to think you are a sleaze, but don't do so to the point that your opening becomes a long apology.

Telling all robs the trial of drama and surprise. Consider teases, as in, "Next week on Survivor." There is a reason that movie trailers are so popular.

"Officer Knowles was the first police officer on the scene. He talked to the defendant who told him something very surprising. Listen carefully to what Knowles says."

Personalize Your Client

Personalization is more than names. Give the jury some feel for who your client is. With thought, you can avoid the resume approach—"Let me tell you something about my client"—by weaving biographical information into the fabric of the story.

"Ms. Worth knew the road well, as she had driven it for the last eight years taking her children to school."

Defendants' Opening Statements

Consider narrowing the issues:

"My client admits that the accident was his fault. The only issue is whether she is permanently disability."

Not only does this make your client sound good, it renders much of the plaintiff's case somewhat irrelevant if not in bad taste. Mary Worth, no doubt, would like to spend most of her time on the strongest part of her case: trashing the defendant. After this opening, if she does, it will seem that she is beating a dead horse. A good opening by the defense can shift focus from an opponent's strengths to her weaknesses.

Consider saying little. It might be a good idea *not* to commit yourself to your defense too early. A *shadow opening* doesn't. Simply talk about burden of proof, the fact that all stories have two sides, and the need to keep an open mind. It may be possible to *reserve* your opening statement until after the plaintiff has rested and it is time for your case. Most lawyers advise against this as they feel it is important for you to get up and say *something* early on.

Consider highjacking the theme. "This case is not about a life ruined by a drunk driver. My opponent worked that phrase into his opening at least three times, as if repetition might hypnotize. When you have heard the evidence, you will realize that this isn't about a life ruined by a drunk; it is about a plaintiff who wants to win the lottery and sit home the rest of her life."

Mistakes

Discussing the Law. Judges get testy if you start instructing the jury as to the law. That's their job. If you feel you need to discuss the law in any detail, check with the judge or court personnel first.

Discussing Inadmissible Evidence. If you are unsure about whether you will be able to get some evidence in, ask for a pretrial ruling so that you know its status before you open.

Overstatement. Don't promise what you cannot deliver. Your opponent will be writing down what you promise and, if you don't produce, will gleefully point this out during closing.

Opening Doors. If you have successfully suppressed your client's confession, don't open the door to its introduction by stating "There will be no evidence that my client confessed." Don't open the door to evidence your opponent could otherwise not introduce by making an assertion that can only be met with that evidence.

Argument. Everyone knows that *you cannot argue during opening*. Few, however, know what argument actually is. We are a tad shaky ourselves.

> *"We will prove X, Y, and Z and, from those facts, you will conclude that the defendant was negligent."*

Technically, "argument" is the drawing of inferences and conclusions from "facts". It is argument because differing inferences and conclusions are possible. However "facts" are essentially meaningless without some knowledge of why they might be relevant.

"Take I 40 East from Flagstaff" isn't much of a road map without knowing you're heading to Albuquerque.

There is an unspoken convention that *it's not nice to object* during *opening* or *closing* unless things are terrible. You can rely on this convention, plus confusion as to what argument is, to get away with some argument during opening. However there are clear cases: emotional appeals for justice, discussions of the need to "send messages," and, operatic death scenes.

Delivery

Conversation, talking with a friend about an important matter, trumps high oratory. Talk to a juror in the back row to assure proper voice level and eye contact.

Silence is effective. A pause underlines a point and allows the jury to reflect. Consider beginning your opening with a short pause. This will allow the jurors to settle in and focus on you.

Use exhibits if you can. Some are visual learners. "What's the use of a book without pictures?" PowerPoint presentations might help. Actors state their intention before going on stage; it blocks stage fright and the perennial worry of what to do with one's hands. Try this:

> *"My intention is to help the jury understand this case from the perspective of my client."*

DIRECT: TELLING STORIES

Have a list of your two or three (occasionally more) main points and the order of you will make them. Consider "drawing the sting" and the dangers of "opening the door". Warn the witness to avoid "hearsay" and "speculation" and of appearing partisan by volunteering damaging material on direct or trying to explain away harmful material on cross. Explain you can clear up any misimpressions on redirect and warn against answering too quickly during cross and looking at you for help.

If you have done on all this, read on. If not, go back and review prior chapters.

Trying a law suit is essentially telling a story, most probably from your client's perspective. How can you tell one that is clear, believable, and dramatic?

Develop a simple theme that fits the facts and your legal theory. Trials are made up of bits and pieces of information. Trials can be like paintings that can't be appreciated until one steps back and sees the whole. You want the jury to, eventually, see the whole of your client's story. What keeps their interest tethered is your theme. Themes should simple and create an emotional filter through which the jury can process your client's story. Themes should be stated as early as jury selection and repeated frequently throughout the trial so that the jury takes that theme with them to the jury room.

"She done him wrong."

"Doctors aren't miracle workers."

"Nobody should have to live in fear."

"Pinocchio is a liar."

Once you have a theme, you are ready to tell the story.

Telling a Clear Story

Unless you are scattering bits and pieces to gather up in a brilliant closing argument (a plan which seldom works), you will want the jury to understand what the witness is saying. Sculp the testimony, don't just present it: use *introductions and transitions* and consider proceeding *by topic*, not chronologically. And remember to reinforce your theme.

Introductions and Transitions

Take *Hansel and Gretel*, the *Hadley v. Baxendale* of child abandonment law. The children have testified that, after dinner on September 1, they overheard their stepmother and father planning to abandon them in the Black Forest. You are defending the stepmother, fulfilling the highest ethical standard of our profession. She is your first witness.

> *"Directing your attention to the evening of September 1, tell the jury what you did after dinner."*

Unless jurors recall that the alleged conspiracy occurred on the first they will not see why this is important. With a flare of drama:

> Q: *You were in the courtroom when Hansel testified.*
>
> A: *Yes.*
>
> Q: *What did he say about the evening of September 1?*
>
> A: *That I conspired with my husband to leave him in the Dark Forest.*
>
> Q: *Did you?*
>
> A: *No. I wasn't home. It was a Thursday and on Thursdays I spend the entire evening as a Hospice volunteer.* (You never bothered to hear her side, did you? That's why we defend the despised!)

Another solution is to simply introduce the topic:

> Q: *Ms. Stepmother, the first area I would like to explore with you is whether you and your husband conspired to abandon the children. There has been an allegation made that you did so on September 1. Tell the jury what really happened?*

After she denies the conspiracy a long pause on your part would let it sink in.

Transitions prune irrelevant testimony. Suppose you have two facts you want to establish with the witness, that she saw the Chevy run the red light and, when the ambulance arrived 20 minutes later, she heard the driver of the Chevy admit fault.

After establishing the running of the red light, ever fearful of the infamous leading question, one might ask, "What, if anything, happened next?'' With this question, it will take about ten minutes of irrelevant testimony (a crowd gathered, flares were put out, traffic was rerouted) to get to the point of the ambulance arriving. Instead, why not:

''Now, sometime after the crash, did an ambulance arrive?''

Another way to avoid the march through the irrelevancies is to advise the witness that when you ask, ''What happened after the crash?'' she should relate the arrival of the ambulance and skip the intervening events. The problem is that the witness will come off coached and partisan, jumping for the jugular without prompting. *Use transitions, not rehearsals.*

Proceed by Topic

Usually it is easier to understand a story if it is told chronologically.

Q: *Officer, when you first arrived at the scene, what happened?*

A: *Blah, blah, blah happened.*

Q: *And what happened next?*

(Three years of law school for this?) However, clarity might be improved proceeding by topic. All you have to do is give up the safety of ''What happened next?''

The witness saw the accident and then later heard the defendant's statement. Say that you want to end with the accident, not the conversation. Child's play.

Q: *You were at the scene of the accident?*

Q: *Were you there when the ambulance arrived?*

Q: *Did you hear anything the defendant said?*

Q: *Returning to the time of the accident. What did you see?*

Simplify

The shorter, the less cluttered, the more understandable the message. Use three witnesses, not eight; make three points, not ten, have the witness testify in twenty minutes, not thirty. Some lawyers, most often prosecutors, over try their cases. Fearful they might lose, they put on everything. The danger is jury boredom and resentment, not to mention that the telling points are buried in a sea of facts.

Demonstrative Evidence

"What's the use of a book without pictures?" asked Alice. There are many academic careers devoted to establishing the self-evident, that seeing is believing. Would an exhibit, or computer generated display or demonstration help the jury understand your point? Get your witness off the stand using a chart, demonstrating a motion, making a diagram.

Rehearse if you are going to have a witness write on a board or demonstrate something. A defendant's expert was asked to demonstrate why it was impossible for the defendant's knife to cause the victim's wounds. Fidgeting with the knife for a while, then "By George, if he held it like this."

The Problem of Filler

> *"I am a checkout clerk at the supermarket. The defendant walked in and pulled a gun."*

That seems clear enough but *only* because we have filled in the missing details. We see the defendant come into *our* store. Maybe at our store the checkout clerk couldn't have had that good a look. Throwing more testimony might not solve the problem.

> *"Well, there are six registers, and off to the left is where they keep the tomatoes."*

A diagram of the store would be worth a thousand words. Be aware that the details that your witness doesn't supply will be supplied by the jury and they are most likely wrong.

Telling Believable Stories

What makes this witness believable?

Is there anything about the witness that would lead the jury to trust him? Let the witnesses tell the jury who they are, where they live, what they do. To steal a line from Oscar Levant, hopefully not:

> *"When I was young I looked like Al Capone, but I lacked his compassion."*

Don't introduce your witnesses with leading questions. Allow them to get comfortable talking. You need not front load all of this information but rather disclose some down steam: "I know the road well because I take it driving my children to school."

What makes the witness unbelievable? You have warned them against being too partisan and trying to explain away everything that hurts. The witness may have obvious bias and perhaps has made prior inconsistent statements. Consider drawing the sting, either in your opening or during the testimony.

Ask Good Questions

Avoid leading and vague questions. *Leading* witnesses through key testimony prevents them from telling their story and *vague questions* answered in damning ways create the appearance of bias. Experienced lawyers may not bail you out by objecting.

Bored and uninterested send bad vibes. Before your ask your first question, recite:

> *"It is very important for me to hear what this witness has to say."*

Lay firm Foundations

Non-expert witnesses can testify only to what they saw, heard, felt, tasted, or smelled but, *before* they can, it must be shown that they were in a position to see, hear, feel, taste or smell. That is known as *foundation.*

In an intersection case, an eye witness is asked:

> Q: *What color was the light when the defendant entered the intersection?*

The defense lawyer might object, "lack of foundation." The mere fact that she was at the scene of the accident does not mean that she was in a position to see the color of the light. Lay good foundations even if your adversary doesn't insist on it.

> Q: *Before the accident, could you see the intersection?*
>
> A: *Yes. I was walking towards it.*
>
> Q: *How far from the intersection were you?*
>
> A: *Not that far. From about here to the back of the Courtroom.*
>
> Q: *From your position, could you see both the defendant's car and the color of the light?*
>
> A: *Yes, I was walking toward the light and I saw the defendant's car on my left.*
>
> Q: *Did anything call your attention to the intersection right before the accident?*

A: I was watching it, hoping to cross before it turned red.

Q: Did you see the color of the light as the defendant's car entered the intersection?

A: Yes.

Q: What color was it?

A: Red.

Show Details

While memory research establishes that the presence of details does not always mean truthfulness, details convince others.

Q: Did you observe the defendant exit his vehicle just after the collision?

A: Yes, I did.

Q: Were you able to form an opinion as to his sobriety?

A: Yes. He was drunk.

But how can we be sure the witness came to the right conclusion?

Q: Did you observe the defendant exit his vehicle just after the collision?

A: Yes, I did.

Q: Where were you in relation to him?

A: I was standing on the curb, about five feet from the driver's door. He got out of that door.

Q: Was there anything interfering with your perception?

A: No.

Q: How was he attired?

A: He had a T-shirt on with a picture of a tiger. Under the tiger, it said "I never met a man I didn't like."

Q: What was the defendant's condition?

A: His eyes were bloodshot, his clothes were messed up. I noticed a strong smell of alcohol, and when he asked, "Is this the way to Pismo Beach?" his speech was slurred. He could barely stand up.

Q: *How do you know he could barely stand up?*

A: *Well, when he got out of the car, he leaned on the door. When he walked off, I saw him almost fall twice.*

Q: *Do you have an opinion as to his sobriety?*

A: *Yes. He was drunk.*

The message is the same: the defendant was drunk. Legally, both versions are proper: a lay witness can form an opinion as to sobriety. Both are *understandable*. But when the time comes for the jury to sort out all the bits of testimony it has heard, the longer version is much more likely to be *recalled*. And *believed*. With all the supporting details, the jury knows he was drunk without being told.

The only problem with the longer version is the graduate school vocabulary:

Q: *Did you observe the defendant exit his vehicle after the collision?*

How about:

Q: *Did you see the defendant get out of his car after the wreck?*

Lawyers, warned of the dangers of talking legal jargon, talk graduate school. If you are not in a rush, go over the transcript and edit it to, say, college grad.

Tell Dramatic Stories

Ask questions as if the answers mattered

When you first interviewed the witness, you were on the edge of your seat; the next couple of answers could make or break your case. Recapture that excitement.

Draw out and repeat key testimony

Q: *What did you find when you searched the defendant's house?*

A: *Some cocaine, scales, marijuana, baggies, and a lot of twenties.*

Would Hollywood do this? Of course not. In the movies the climatic scenes are shown up close and in slow motion: the murder knife descending, the basketball bouncing on the rim, the car careening toward the guard rail. For key testimony, slow it down so the jury can *see* it.

> *Q: When you first entered the house, what did you do?*
>
> *A: We called out to see if anyone was there. Then, with our weapons drawn, we checked the house to see if anyone was there. Once we had more or less secured the house, we began our search.*
>
> *Q: What was the first room you searched?*
>
> *A: Well, a room in the back. A spare bedroom. It wasn't being used as a bedroom. More of a work room. The shades were drawn so the room was dark. When we opened the blinds, light flooded in.*
>
> *Q: What did you then see?*

Go slowly. Involve the jury. Let them see the scene. Let them hold their breath. Will the knife find its mark? Will the ball go in? Even if we know it will go in, watching it bounce on the rim is still riveting.

Repetitions are fine. Remember, the jury has not heard this tale before. You cannot ask the *same* question, time and time again, or you will face an *"Asked and Answered"* objection. So ask different questions getting at the same fact.

> *Q: You say you found cocaine? How do you know it was cocaine?*
>
> *Q: Where exactly did you find the cocaine?*
>
> *Q: What was the cocaine wrapped in?*

Silence and Confrontations

Silence builds suspense. Dropping you voice to a whisper to ask a key question focuses attention.

Another way to enliven the testimony is with *confrontations*.

> *Q: Mrs. Stepmother, is that Hansel sitting in the back of the court?*
>
> *A: Yes.*
>
> *Q: Did you plot with your husband to kill him?*
>
> *A: Are you kidding? Plot with that nincompoop?*

CROSS EXAMINATION

Q: Let's see now. Oh, yes. Are you really, really, sure that it was my client you saw and not somebody else?

A: Yes.

Q: Cross your fingers, hope to die?

What do you want from the witness? Information? A perception of bias? Of stupidity? Of deception?

What is your purpose? Once you have a purpose, you can put together a plan.

Decide what you want and avoid *pointless cross*; the witness who killed you on direct will testify *twice*. The longer you cross-examine without scoring, the more believable the witness.

"I have no questions of *this* witness, Your Honor," with a shrug suggesting that the witness has not hurt you and is beneath the contempt of civilized folk. *Shadow cross* is another option. No cross at all might suggest to the jury that you accept all of the witness's testimony. Ask a few harmless questions and sit down.

The second mistake is *failing to listen*. Pause, count to 3 after each answer. Has the witness answered or deflected your question? Should you pursue new avenues opened by the deflection or force the witness to answer the original question? Be nimble, be quick.

Cross need not be *cross*. Beating up witnesses often doesn't play well with the jury and alienating the witness may close down areas of fruitful examination.

Remember that the more the witness ducks your questions, tries to explain away problems with his testimony, the worse he looks. You may feel that you aren't in control of the witness but that's fine if he's self-destructing.

There are four basic things you can do on cross:

1. *Help* your case by having the witness corroborate some of your contentions;
2. *Confront* the witness with your theory;

3. *Undermine* the adverse testimony by discrediting the *witness*;

4. *Undermine* the adverse testimony by discrediting the *testimony*.

These are not mutually exclusive and, indeed, it is possible to accomplish all four in one examination, particularly in your dreams.

Helping Your Case

"Ladies and Gentlemen of the Jury, even my opponent's witnesses agree that it was a dark and stormy night."

What facts *must* the witness admit which will support your case?

What facts *might* the witness admit which will support your case?

The facts the witness *must* admit are those testified to on direct.

Q: On direct, you testified that it was a dark and stormy night, isn't that right?

Highlight favorable testimony. It is OK to go over the same material on cross that was developed on direct; "asked and answered" only applies to the *same* lawyer asking the same question.

You are on fairly safe ground if the witness has previously given the answer you want in a deposition or report. But what if you just don't know what the answer will be?

Asking questions not knowing the answer

In the lore of trial advocacy the advice is "Never!" This advice is supported by wonderful stories where the lawyer asked such a question and had the case blow up. However one has to wonder, if the answer was that devastating, why wasn't it elicited on direct? Paul Bergman in his fine book of trial practice advises that, if the desired answer would be key, you might risk the question provided that you have other evidence to disprove the bad answer. Of course in an ideal world you would have asked the question during discovery and would not be faced with the choice.

Beyond the scope of direct

In many jurisdictions you can cross examine only as to matters testified to on direct. Say that the eye-witness, who testified only to the accident itself, overheard, two days later, the defendant making a damaging admission. Can you bring this out on cross? That testimony would go "beyond the scope of direct" and in some jurisdictions that's taboo. Usually this is not much of a problem because you can call the witness as part of your case. The only downside is that as the witness will now be yours on direct, you cannot ask leading questions *except* if the witness is hostile and you get the court's permission to treat her as such.

Experts and Roads Not Taken

With condescending pomposity the expert testifies, "I did test 'X' and my scientific conclusion is 'Y'." The jury will hate her but probably will believe her. And she might destroy you if you attack the core of her testimony by attempting to show test 'X' is invalid or that she performed test 'X' improperly. Pomposity attests to competence. A better strategy is to develop the negatives.

> Q: *To find 'Y', one could also conduct test 'A', isn't that a fact?*
>
> Q: *And test 'A', is as reliable as test 'X'?*
>
> Q: *Test 'B' is also recognized in the scientific community as a valid and reliable test to find 'Y', isn't that right?*
>
> Q: *And so with test 'C'?*
>
> Q: *Now, from a scientific point of view, the more tests you run which give you the same result, the more sure you are of your conclusion, isn't that correct?*
>
> Q: *In reaching your conclusion of "Y," did you conduct test "A?"*

Confronting the Witness

> Q: *Hansel, isn't it a fact that there were no bread crumbs, no witch, no chicken bone, and that you made all of this up because your stepmother won't let you play with Jack and Jill?*

A horrible compound question. Remember: *one fact, one question*. Break the question into specifics: crumbs, witches, chicken bones.

Unless you're Perry Mason, you'll get denials. So what? Sometimes all you can do is confront the witness with your theory, signaling the jury that you do not accept the testimony and reminding them of your side. Further fair play and good drama generally require that, before you attempt to prove your accusations as part of your case, you should make them, face to face.

In this regard, it is *ethically improper* to ask an accusatory question ("When did you stop kicking your puppy?") unless you have a good faith basis to believe the accusation.

Discrediting the Witness

Impeachment Showing Bias. Bias can result from a relationship with one of the parties (mother), an interest in the outcome (jailhouse snitch), or simply money (experts). Often your adversary will call attention to these factors in direct in the hopes of drawing the sting. On cross you can revisit the issue.

Q: Now you love your son, isn't that right?

Q: And you are worried that he might go to jail?

Q: If he goes to jail, you will have a hard time visiting him?

Impeachment Showing Mistake. Using slash and burn, which we will describe momentarily, you might be able to trip up the perjurer on the details of the testimony. It is harder to do so with a witness who is simply mistaken. They believe the details because they have witnessed a similar event and simply have confused it or because they reached a conclusion and filled in the missing details to support it. Rather than trying to trip them up on details explore possible sources of their error.

Q: Have you witnessed similar events, either in person or on TV?

Q: Have you discussed this with other folks? Read any newspaper articles on it?

Eye-witnesses are impeached by showing that they might be mistaken. Shadows and movement can cause mistakes in perception as can one's mental state (confusion, distraction, fear, drunkenness).

Eye-witnesses in criminal cases are particularly problematic. Juries believe them more than other evidence. Unfortunately they are often wrong; studies showing about 30% of the time. If the identification came after a line-up, photographic or regular, ask whether it was double blind (the police officer, not knowing which the suspect is, could not affect the decision) and whether the witness was told that the suspect may not be in the line-up (thus eliminating "pretty sures"). If it was a photo lineup, were the pictures shown one at a time? Showing them as a group might lead to "most likely". Prosecutors, wishing not to convict the innocent, should insist on these two requirements.

Impeachment with Prior Inconsistent Statements. Some trials are conducted as if the *only* thing the lawyers learned in three long years was the doctrine of prior inconsistent statements. Jurors know, even if lawyers don't, that we are all inconsistent some of the time. Don't impeach with prior statements just because you learned how.

Important prior inconsistent statements are very useful. We reviewed how to impeach with prior statements in our chapter on questions. (Or maybe we didn't.)

Impeaching Experts

Being paid? Always on the same side, insurance companies or grieving widows and suffering orphans? Take a careful look at their resumes; many fudge their qualifications. Finally remember what we said in our chapter on mistakes: 30% of scientific papers contain errors or report results that cannot be repeated. What kind of expert are they? The best eye surgeon in the world is not qualified to talk about what optometrists should or should not know.

Discrediting the Story

Going after Collateral Details

Sometimes direct will be a tale told by an idiot and you will have enough to work with by stressing inconsistencies and improbabilities. However if the story holds together on its own you must look for collateral matters which may throw it into doubt.

> *If the situation was as testified, what else would have happened? What else would not have happened?*
>
> *If the witness saw the accident well enough to testify she did, what else would she have seen? What would she not have seen? What would she have done? What would she have not done?*

To put it in a more confusing way:

> *If X is true, then Y must be or is likely to be true. (Your job, prove Y false).*
>
> *If X is true, then Z must be or is likely to be false. (Your job, prove Z true).*

While you can prove these matters elsewhere in your case, you might try to use cross to force the witness to admit Y is false or Z is true. This will take stealth. Witnesses want to protect their testimony and if they sense you are about to blow it up will admit to nothing . Close off escape routes or try slash and burn.

Closing off escape routes

If confronted with an inconvenient fact, how might the witness explain it away? A police officer didn't include an important fact in her police report."Everything doesn't go in the report. I was busy that night." Close these escapes. Close them before you ask about anything substantive.

> Q: *You did a good job investigating this event, isn't that right?*
>
> Q: *You weren't distracted or too tired, or too busy, to do a good job?*
>
> Q: *You know that police reports are very important, fellow police officers, prosecutors and even judges may rely on them, correct?*
>
> Q: *And while you can't put everything in a report, you will put the important things in the report?*
>
> Q: *And if a defendant admits to starting a fight, you would agree with me that that is important?*

As this is a happy book, before popping the question, close the escape routes.

> Q: *Now, you're not already married, isn't that right?*
>
> Q: *And you're not in love with anyone else, isn't that a fact?*
>
> Q: *And we're not first cousins, correct?*

The other way to prevent the witness from knowing where you are going, not recommended outside the courtroom, is "slash and burn."

Slash and Burn

Jump around from topic to topic, hoping to force the witness into a contradiction or into asserting a fact that is either clearly wrong or easily shown to be. The basic technique is to ask, rapid-fire, a series of questions which force a series of "yes" or "no" answers, keeping the witness off balance. Your questions must be very focused and should contain only one fact. Unfocused and compound questions call for longer answers.

There is no need to snarl. This technique works due to disorder and speed, not tone. Ask a question with accusation in your voice, dollars to donuts you'll get a "No."

The theory is that liars have a hard time keeping their stories straight. But so too do elderly folks, young folks, and pretty much all of us. Don't misuse the technique.

Your opponent will have probably warned the witness of the technique and advised her to take some time before answering the question. During trial, your opponent will break you flow with:

"I object, the lawyer is not allowing the witness time to think."

Some learn better by tight logical prose, others by stories. Dog stories. The dog's lawyer jumps up:

I object, your Honor, the examining lawyer is purposefully confusing Shadow by going back and forth between people years and dog years.

Jack Benny was on Bob Hope's show and was being ripped by him. "You could never get away with that," he responded, "if my writers were here." Well you writers won't be there so don't expect cross to go as well as it does on TV; realize that it might make your case a lot worse. Never forget that you have Closing Argument to make most, if not all, of the points you want to make. And it is safer than trying to make them on cross; your writers *will be* there.

CLOSING ARGUMENT, NO CONVERSATION

Closing arguments are really, really fun. Intense. Exhilarating. It is only you and the jurors. You'll soar.

Don't worry. It's OK if you forget a key point (a juror will think of it), and it's OK if you don't carry off, with great aplomb, all of the clever ploys suggested by folks like us. Jurors take their jobs seriously and decide cases on evidence, not on theatrics.

It is your opportunity to tell the story that has come out in bits and pieces during trial, in the clutter of questions, objections and sidebars. It is your opportunity to explain to the jury what it all means. And you will be able to tell it without interruption provided you do not stumble by misstating the evidence, vouching for witnesses ("I know she is telling the truth") or urging the jury to "send a message" to drug dealers, evil corporations or greedy widows. Provided further, of course, your opponent is not a jerk objecting to break your flow.

When you tell the story, give jurors what they need to decide in your favor. As Dr. Donald E. Vincent, a noted jury psychologist said in *Jury Persuasion*:

> *Jury persuasion is a strategic activity—one which is dependant upon the trial lawyer's ability to conceive, craft, and articulate messages with which the jury will agree.*

There are infinite ways to tell a story so we offer some general thoughts. Best to tell the story from the perspective of your client; active voice is better than passive, present tense better than past, verbs and nouns better than adverbs and adjectives. Analogies and metaphors work, except stale ones ("He looked liked something the cat drug in.") Emotions are important. Remember most people base most decisions on what feels right; they use reason to justify the rightness. But you can't impose feelings like a revival preacher. When jurors leave they go to *deliberate, not vote.* Your arguments must have staying power; most emotional outbursts, smoke and mirrors last, what, five minutes. Summation should be evocative. Evoke [subtly] the emotions jurors were feeling as they heard the evidence.

What about style? "Argument" may send the wrong message. It is probably better to think of your closing as a "conversation," your last opportunity to talk to the jury about why your client should win. Respect the jury. Don't try to fool them or rush them to judgment. Appreciate the tough job they face. Help them think things through.

Usually this isn't an opportunity to change minds. Television to the contrary, very few cases are won or lost on the basis of closing argument. The jurors, if they have not already decided, are leaning one way or the other. Most advertising is designed not to recruit new customers but to reassure current ones. So too most closings.

Don'ts

Don't ramble

Know when to shut up. Jurors are people too, the trial is over and they want to deliberate. Except in long complex cases, no more than 30 minutes.

Don't misstate the evidence

It's likely you will.

"I'll be discussing the evidence. Maybe what I say is not exactly how you remember it. Go with your memory, not mine. I'm not trying to confuse you or mislead you. But sometimes, like everyone, I make mistakes."

Don't use rebuttal for new arguments

If you have the burden of proof you will have the last argument to "rebut" what your opponent argued in closing. It is bush, and objectionable, to introduce new arguments at this stage; your opponent has no opportunity to respond.

Don't fail to connect with your theme

Repetition is why advertising works.

Don't fail to object when you should

Everyone is entitled to his own opinion but not to his own facts. To preserve your record, object if your opponent is misstating the evidence. She is entitled to her own opinion as to what those facts prove so you cannot object to her flights of fancy; that is what your rebuttal is for. The only downside of objecting is getting overruled: if the lawyer is doing things that strike you as wrong, even though you may not have a label to apply, object. Maybe the judge will help you out.

Of course to object you first have to listen. Many beginners more or less collapse after they have closed and don't listen to the rebuttal thus waiving appeals on such bases as "beyond to scope" of rebuttal.

Choices

Organization

Should you start with your case and then attack your opponent's? In presenting your case does it make sense to go chronologically or by topic? Which witness will you discuss first? Whatever order you choose, always be able to answer two questions:

1. *How* might you have organized it differently?
2. *Why* is your scheme better than the alternatives?

Opening and Closing Riffs

Experts stress *primacy* and *recency*: what we hear first, and last, make the biggest impression.

> *"Ladies and Gentlemen of the Jury, I would first like to thank you for your attention during the trial."*

Yuck. If you mean it, thank them later.

People have to settle in. Thanking the jury, like the stale dinner joke, focuses attention but doesn't grab it. "You know, folks, I just heard a good one. This dog goes into a bar, sits down, and orders a scotch and toilet water."

Silence is a better alternative. Approach the podium, look at the jury, and say nothing. After 30 seconds, the audience is yours. Whispers work too. Bellow and everyone sits back and gets a tad lazy; speak softly and everyone leans forward and concentrates.

The problem with the "thank you for your attention" opening is that it totally lacks pizzaz. What is the most important thing you want to tell the jurors? Tell them.

"My client will never walk again."

"The widgets sucked!"

Work hard on your closing riff. It will get you off stage gracefully. One possibility is to come back to your opening—

symmetry is always nice. Or consider leaving the jury with a haunting sentence, or question, or image.

Joseph Ellis ends *Founding Brothers* with the death of John Adams. Adams knew that his long time enemy/friend, Thomas Jefferson, would become history's darling and that he, Adams, would be pretty much forgotten. Adams is on his death bed; unbeknownst to him, Jefferson had died a matter of hours earlier. *"Thomas Jefferson still lives,"* were Adam's last words. Ellis ends his book with:

"Adams was wrong for the moment, but right for the ages."

Concessions v. Taking No Prisoners

"My opponent has proved Z." Smart move or fool's errand? Concessions make you seem reasonable and trustworthy. However "You never can tell!" Perhaps there are a couple of jurors who aren't convinced as to Z and now can't argue it during deliberations. Should you argue only points you believe in? The case for honesty is that people usually pick up insincerity. On the other hand, you never can tell.

Opening the door for jurors

They may be issues that jurors are reluctant to discuss and it is your job to start the conversation. Some personal injury lawyers don't name a figure hoping that the jury will run amuck. However, if they don't name a large figure, jurors may be reluctant to do so. Similarly, jurors are reluctant to call people liars. If you believe opposition witnesses lied, call them liars; if you are reluctant, so too will be jurors.

Consider the role of *extremism*. Rather than *"The evidence suggests that the witness was lying,"* why not *"The witness is a lying, perjuring, genocidal racist."* This will make your supporters on the jury appear reasonable "OK, not Hitler but surely a run of the mill racist and perjurer." If you are too extreme, however, you lose credibility. There must be some suggestion that the witness is a racist; don't use the attack on Barney.

Telling the jurors what to conclude or leaving it up to them

Say that you want the jury to conclude that a person was drunk. Your supporting facts are the testimony as to his slurred speech, as to the smell of alcohol on his breath, and as to his embarrassingly garbled refrains from *The Man of La Mancha*. You can argue:

"We know he was drunk because A, B, an C."

This is an explicit argument, telling the jury what to conclude from the evidence. This helps pull things together. However, you could also simply argue

"Remember A, B, and C."

and let the jurors come to their own conclusion. People don't like being told what to think and when they come to their own conclusions they will own and defend them. Hit the jurors on the head over and over with your conclusions leaves them with the impression that you think they're idiots.

Eye Contact and Notes

Thinking of closing argument as a conversation is helpful but it is a one-way conversation; your audience can't ask for clarification or tell you they disagree. Arguing Point X. What are the possibilities?

1. The jurors already agree with Point X, arguing it further wastes time.
2. The jurors don't buy Point X and never will, arguing further, wastes time and undercuts your credibility.
3. The jurors aren't convinced of Point X and need further explanation.

Some lawyers believe that they can read the jury, crossed arms indicating rejection. We're generally not convinced: crossed arms might indicate "I agree with Point X, but I hate to." Our best advice is to maintain eye contact with the jurors, to be open to the possibility that you aren't as clear as you think, that you may be wasting time arguing Point X, and be willing to edit on the fly.

Look at the jury, and not at your notes, but don't stay focused on one juror too long; many people become quite uncomfortable—Should I smile? Nod? Look away? Others may feel left out.

Have notes, not as a script but as a security blanket. Some lawyers try to memorize their closing so they won't need notes, the theory being that the jurors will become convinced that the lawyer has a terrific memory and recalls prior testimony better than they. However it may well be that the jurors aren't listening but thinking, "Look, Mom, no hands."

Practice your Closing

Just don't think about what your are going to say. Get up and say it. Better to try it out in front of a neutral party to get feedback. Best to try it out on a non-lawyer. [If you only have friends who are lawyers, that's a problem for another book].

All of this might be overwhelming. Suddenly you find yourself in a courtroom, on center stage, and you can't remember your opening lines, only that this is supposed to be really, really fun. Relax. The worst that can happen is that you will have a wonderful story to tell (eventually). But we can't close on a down note. We have all been where you are, fearful of being unable to pull it off. A philosopher wrote of his fear of entering a field dominated by intellectual giants.

> *"I have been lost in admiration but I have not lost courage. I have said with Correggio, 'I too am a painter!' "*

What a great quote to end the chapter. What a great quote to end a short and happy guide.

> *You will be lost in admiration but don't lose courage. You too are a lawyer!*

†